Making Virtuous Daughters and Wives

Making Virtuous Daughters and Wives

An Introduction to Women's Brata Rituals in Bengali Folk Religion

June McDaniel

STATE UNIVERSITY OF NEW YORK PRESS

Cover photo: "Singing to the goddess Tushu," by James Denosky.
Courtesy of James Denosky.

Published by
State University of New York Press, Albany

© 2003 State University of New York

For information, address State University of New York Press,
90 State Street, Suite 700, Albany, NY 12207

Production by Dana Foote
Marketing by Jennifer Giovani

Library of Congress Cataloging-in-Publication Data

McDaniel, June.
    Making virtuous daughters and wives : an introduction to women's Brata rituals in
Bengali folk religion / June McDaniel.
        p.   cm.
    Includes bibliographical references and index.
    ISBN 0–7914–5565–3 (alk. paper)—ISBN 0–7914–5566–1 (pbk. : alk. paper)
    1. Vratas.   2. Hinduism—Rituals.   3. Bengali (South Asian people)—
Folklore.   4. Folklore—India—West Bengal.   5. Hindu women—India—West
Bengal—Religious life.   6. West Bengal (India)—Religious life and customs.
BL1237.78 .M32 2003
294.5'38—dc21

                                                                          2002030542

10 9 8 7 6 5 4 3 2 1

Contents

Acknowledgments

I would like to thank the Fulbright Program, whose Senior Scholar Research Fellowship made it possible for me to do this research in West Bengal, and the College of Charleston, who granted me a year's leave for field research. In India, I would like to thank Satyakam Sengupta, Pashupati Mahato, Soumen Dutta, Asha and Bijoy Mukherjee, Sabujkoli Sen, and the many people from all walks of life who were willing to speak with a foreign researcher about their beliefs and their lives.

Notes on Spelling, Transliteration, and Pronunciation

The major ritual in this book is most well known according to its Sanskrit spelling, or *vrata*. However, it is spelled *brata* is this book, following local Bengali use and pronunciation. Some quotes about the ritual spell the word as *vrata,* and I have left those spellings in the quotes. Thus, the rituals are sometimes called *brata*s, and sometimes *vrata*s. I hope that this is not too confusing to the readers.

We also see several of the brata goddesses called "Mother." This is a title of respect, and also a recognition of a family tie between the worshiper and the goddess—thus, she cannot turn the petitioner away, for he or she is family.

The use of diacritical marks is limited in this book, as it is intended for a broad audience. Thus, many Sanskrit and Bengali terms are spelled phonetically. While this is less authentic to traditional scholarly style, it results in much less mispronunciation of terms by people new to the religions of India, which is a great virtue.

We should note that most words in Bengali with an "s" in them are pronounced with a "sh" sound. Thus, Sasthi is pronounced "Shashthi," Manasa is "Manasha," and so on. Some words spelled with an "s" are pronounced "sh" throughout India, such as Śakti (such pronunciation is described by diacritical marks, which I am largely omitting in this book). For a good Bengali accent, one should also pronounce most "a" sounds as "aw."

Introduction

This is a book about folk religion, the most popular type of religion of the majority of people who live in rural India. Folk religion is a type of mainstream Hinduism, without its focus on caste and purity rules and devotion to pan-Indian deities. Folk religion seeks to fulfill the basic needs of life—health and wealth and a good marriage—and as such it should be the sort of religion most familiar to readers from other, non-Indian traditions.

However, oddly, it is not. This is at least partly because much literature on folk religion emphasizes such older anthropological categories as animism, fetishism, and totemism, as well as the activities of local specialists in ritual worship and trance states. In this small book, I hope to make folk religion in India a bit more familiar and concrete.

When I teach Hinduism in college classes, I cover a variety of subtypes: Vedic, Vedantic, Yogic, Tantric, Dharmic, Bhakti, and folk varieties are included. On a recent class test, a student discussed her preferences between these types. She said that Vedanta was too philosophical—nobody likes such abstract things—Yoga took too much effort, Dharma had too many rules to remember, and Tantra was too weird—she didn't like graveyards. She thought Bhakti seemed like a good approach, but you had to pray too much. The best type was folk religion. People in folk religion cared about being healthy, rich, getting a good husband and having children, having lots of food, and good weather. She said that the church that she attended was just like that—everybody wanted health and wealth and an attractive boyfriend or husband, and prayed for passing tests and getting jobs and winning lawsuits, just like in India. She said that the Christianity that she knew was very much like Hindu folk religion.

She had a point, at least in terms of the goals of the practitioners. When academics do comparative religion, we often look at comparative theological notions—ideas of God or gods, theories of mind and emotion, metaethical theory, justifications for behavior and ritual. Some look for variety and richness and common themes between the traditions. Others look for subtle yardsticks by which to measure the superiority of particular traditions. However, many practitioners look for less complex things: Do people in the other religion care about their families? Are there ways to get the god to do what you want, without too much trouble? Do they have ways to get blessings and good luck? Are there ways to become rich and beautiful and important and respected?

The stories and rituals in this book give answers to these questions, in ways understandable to many cultures. Some stories are more specific to Bengali religion, some might seem alien to Westerners, but most have goals that should be clear and familiar. Stories are a traditional way to learn about a culture, and an enjoyable one. These stories give a richness to village life, portraying a natural world full of speaking plants, deities in disguise, and compassionate owls. It is an animistic world of imagination, and adventure, in a world without computer games and videotapes. There is some folklore remaining in the West, relegated to fairy tales and stories of the tooth fairy and the Easter bunny. However, these are not taken seriously by adults, and soon are lost as the child enters the "real" world. The brata tradition has been taken seriously by adults of village India, and the children enter a vivid world in which their experiences can be shared with adults as well as children. The brata stories provide models for ethics, compassion, and caring for others, making virtuous daughters and wives who fulfill the ideals of Hindu female behavior. They combine the traditional morality of the Sanskrit "great tradition" with the bhakti emphasis on the importance of love rather than purity and caste rules, and the folk emphasis on reverence for nature.

A *brata* (or *vrata* in Sanskrit) traditionally involves both story and ritual, taught to young girls in rural India. This book will examine some brata stories and rituals from the state of West Bengal, in northeastern India. However, we shall first give some background on folk religion, using an example of a major Bengali folk goddess and her festival.

1

Folk Hinduism in West Bengal

In the rural areas of India, we see a variety of notions about the nature of gods and goddesses. They are not "high gods," as we see in the pan-Indian brahmanical forms of Hinduism, but rather regional deities, intimately associated with villages and towns. Indeed, some would not be characterized as gods and goddesses by most people, for those supernatural entities given offerings and worship include ghosts, ancestors, water and plant essences, guardian spirits, and disease controllers. We see some overlap of tribal deities, the deities of non-Hindu or semi-Hindu villagers, with the village gods or *gramadevatas* of village Hinduism. These may be field or mountain spirits, or angry ghosts of women who died violent deaths. All of these may be seen in the large area of folk Hinduism. There is no sharp differentiation between the tribal deities, village deities, and gods and goddesses of brahmanical Hinduism. Rather than a polarity, we see a continuum, for these traditions worship many deities in common. Some themes that may be noted in the worship of folk gods and goddesses:

Regionalism: These deities are associated with specific places, temples, fields, and streams. The Kali of one village is not the same as the next village's Kali. One Chandi gives good hunting, another Chandi cures disease. Goddesses are not pan-Indian; they are specific to a person's tribal or caste group, extended family, neighborhood, or village.

Pragmatism: These deities are rarely worshiped in a spirit of pure and abstract devotion. Worship is for a specific end: fertility, good harvest, good weather, cures for diseases. If gods and goddesses are not worshiped, it is well known that they may get irritable, especially when they get hungry.

Human personality: Deities are like human beings, including both their negative and positive sides. They may be impatient, ill-tempered, impulsive, lustful, greedy, and angry, as well as being merciful and benevolent to their worshipers. Sometimes they are jealous gods, who get angry if they are neglected or if their devotees show more attention to other deities.

Variation of form: Gods and goddesses can be shape-shifters, appearing as natural objects at one time and as human beings at another. One's grandmother may be who she claims to be, or she may be some sort of goddess in

1

disguise. Supernatural power appears in various figures: nature spirits, ghosts, ancestors, regional deities. Gods and goddesses are not limited to disincarnate entities incarnated in statues or particular places. Some gods and goddesses were once people, or are even now transformed people.

Lack of concern for caste: Local gods and goddesses are frequently worshiped by village headmen or non-brahmin priests, as well as priestesses. While the pan-Indian, brahmanical deities require obedience to ritual purity and caste rules, folk deities may be satisfied with worship by people of any ritual or social status.

Some of the most important aspects of folk religion involve the worship of deities (especially goddesses) in natural objects, worship in festivals and by songs, and individual or small-group worship by means of *bratas*, in which people follow a vow and perform ritual action, and listen to a story about the deity. This book will give some examples of the first two aspects, and then focus on the third one.

In folk Hinduism, goddesses are particularly important. Goddesses tend to be aniconic—the goddess might manifest in a stone, in a lake, an unusual tree, or a pile of earth or cowdung. They dwell within nature, without a sculpted human form. This opposes the mainstream Hindu tendency to craft the goddess into statues and images that are recognizably human and are offered incense and flowers and sweets. Folk goddesses are generally believed to appear of their own accord in natural objects and sacred places rather than responding to ritual calls. Goddesses may desire worship, but they are ultimately independent of human wishes and follow their own inclinations.

Folk goddesses may be upwardly mobile, dwelling in a rock in a field, having that rock moved to a sacred grove, and then to an altar in its own hut. With Hindu influence it may move into a small temple, then a larger temple, and then get a statue who is its alter ego. In some rural temples, goddess statues can be seen in classic Hindu form—but at the goddess' feet is the stone from which she arose, and where some aspect of her remains. In other temples, the goddess who showed herself in the great banyan tree is still worshiped at the base of the tree—but also in the temple with the statue. The rock is often a stone slab painted with vermilion and surrounded by offerings. Such rocks are often found as a result of a revelatory dream, or by the request of the goddess, who often appears in the form of an old woman. It is important to respond to such calls, as a family may be punished with disease and death if the goddess calls but is ignored. However, they may be rewarded with wealth and happiness for treating the goddess well, especially feeding and worshiping her.

The worship of goddesses who are believed to dwell within stones and other natural objects is widespread. Many rural goddess temples in West Bengal have been built because of a call from the goddess. A stone, bas-relief, or statue is found in which the goddess is understood by her devotees to dwell, and it is moved to the base of a tree for outside worship, then to a small thatched enclosure (*than*), then to a small building with plaster or cement walls, and then to a full-fledged temple. There are goddesses (and gods) in all of these stages of worship in West Bengal, and the movement from the water to the land is usually understood to be a sort of upward mobility for the goddess. This is because a goddess with a temple and devotees is higher in status than an unknown goddess beneath a pond, whom nobody worships.

There is a common origin story for the stone in which the goddess dwells. A person (usually male) will be asleep at night, and receive a divine call or command in a dream (the Bengali term for this dream command is *svapnadeśa*). It is from a goddess who is generally dissatisfied with her current situation. She is in a lake, pond, or river, or sometimes underground, and she is tired of staying there. She wants to be in a place where she will get more attention, more offerings from devotees, and have more influence on the world. Frequently she complains of being hungry, and not having eaten in several hundred years. Deities without offerings are understood to be starving; as the snake-goddess Manasa tells her worshiper Behula in one of her epic *Manasamangala* poems: "These twelve years, my child, I have been without food. I have spent these twelve years eating the wind."[1]

While the goddess' power may may be found in temples, burning grounds, and other places sacred to the goddess, very frequently it is found in black, rounded stones. Stories along this theme are heard all through rural West Bengal: a person dreams at night of a call from the goddess, who is located in a rock at the bottom of a pond, river or lake. She wishes to get out of the water, and come onto dry land and be worshiped. The person finds the petrified goddess the next morning, sets her up in a shrine, and offers her ritual worship. She is then satisfied, and shows her appreciation by giving miraculous healings and bringing luck.

This set of events is so well known that there is even a "rock scam" described by several urban informants. The goal is wealth, for in India, sanctity can be wealth producing. People offer money to deities hoping for a large return on this relatively small investment, and the person who takes the money is usually the owner or priest of the deity. He is the one who offers access to her.

According to this strategy, a person (or persons) conspires to become the caretaker/owner of a deity in a rock, as a hopefully lucrative career. The person buries a rock with special markings (often a rough figure of a multiarmed Kali or Chandi incised into the stone) near a body of water. After a few weeks or months, he announces a dream to the village, which calls him to dig up a rock in that very place. It was revealed to him in the dream that there is a goddess underground who wishes to be recognized and worshiped. He goes over with a few villagers who later can act as witnesses, digs the rock up, and brings it home. If a confederate from his own or a nearby village can be cured of some chronic health problem (of which he has been visibly complaining for the past few weeks), the caretaker of the deity is employed "in the god business."

There is no further validation needed, because deities are elusive and do not appreciate being tested. Doubters need to be careful—what if the goddess really is in the rock and one is speaking against her? It is a bad idea to get a goddess angry. The goddess in the rock has automatic status. Additionally, temples can become major businesses in towns where there is a scarcity of resources. To doubt a neighbor's vision may also prevent the growth of a major business opportunity and do a disservice to the community.

Most traditional informants said that this simulation must be rare, for the goddess is known to have a quick temper and gets angry at people who try to use her. Thus, even if the village liar were to claim a dream call, it would be likely to be believed, for chancing the goddess' anger is dangerous and the man would have to be mad to do it. Doubting the goddess' call might make her angry, so people should hesitate to be skeptical. Now that Western ideas have penetrated into the most rural of areas, however, we do see a growing skepticism and even denial of the truth of the dream commands. Nevertheless, people still go to the temples, deciding to be on the safe side.

I asked people how the goddess got into the rock in the first place, but was generally met with blank stares: "How are we supposed to know how goddesses do that sort of thing?" Informants willing to deal with this question generally had two speculations; either she was in the rock since the beginning of time, or she entered the rock later on. Those of the eternal school had the goddess in the rock forever, sleeping or dreaming or semicomatose, until one day she awakens and decides that she doesn't like the environment. Either she broadcasts a general call at that point to be taken out and worshiped (and whoever is suitably receptive hears her and comes to rescue her) or she waits for decades or centuries until just the right person comes along (her criteria for the right person are known only to herself). For the more particular goddesses, this may mean years in a quite undignified position. Some rocks are used as laundry stones, where washermen and women come to beat dirty clothes against rocks, some are trod on by low-caste and outcaste people, some are thrown by children and kicked by animals. However, the goddess stoically bears years of pounding by the laundryman's saris and kurta shirts, waiting for her rescuer and her new status as village goddess.

Sometimes goddesses are said to be incarnate in rocks as a result of a curse. An early example of this is the *Ramayana* story of the sage Gautama's wife, Ahalya. The god Indra lusted after the beautiful Ahalya. He took on the illusory form of her husband and slept with her. Despite the fact that she thought she was with her husband, Gautama was nevertheless quite angry, and cursed her to be transformed into a rock until she would be liberated by the god Rama during his incarnation on earth. As the *Adhyatma Ramayana,* a version of the *Ramayana* popular in West Bengal, describes the situation:

> After thus cursing Indra, the chief of celestials, he entered his hermitage, and there saw Ahalya standing, trembling in fear and with palms joined in salu-

tation. Gautama said to her: "O degenerate one! You will be converted into a rock in this Ashrama. Without any food and drink day and night, and subjected to all the inclemencies of weather like rain, sun, wind, etc. you will be stationed here in the practice of severe austerity, meditating on the Supreme Being Rama dwelling in the hearts of all. This place, which has been my hermitage, will hereafter be without any living creature. After you have spent several thousand years in this condition, Sri Rama, the son of Dasaratha, along with his brother Lakshmana will be coming to this place. When he places his feet on the rock, with which you will now gain identity by my curse, you will be freed from sin. You will then adore Rama with great devotion, circumambulating him and prostrating before him. Liberated from the effects of the curse, you will again have opportunity to serve me.[2]

Some informants mentioned a myth of a primordial dismemberment of the goddess at the beginning of the world, a cross between the Purusa Sukta story in the *Rig Veda* and the myth of Sati. The earth was made from the body of the goddess, and some of her body parts were more conscious than others (these became the sacred rocks). Other informants said that the consciousness of the goddess Prakriti (the goddess of matter) is scattered throughout all the world, though more visible in some places than in others.[3]

Those who believed that the goddess' entrance into the rock was a later event had a variety of theories as to why this might have occured. Some informants speculated that perhaps the rock was originally a statue, enlivened by a brahmin priest through the ritual of *prāṇu-pratishthā* (when a deity is called down by mantra to dwell in a statue), but the statue was worn away over time, with the goddess somehow trapped inside. Others stated that there were many invasions throughout Indian history, and the deities fled the invaders just as the town or village inhabitants did, somehow ending up in a rock or tree, or placed to rest by others in Mother Earth. Sometimes she was taken away from a temple in a war zone or area of famine by a fleeing priest; or her caretaker followed her instructions to move her elsewhere and died on the way to her desired locale, and the presence of her statue was unknown or forgotten by others. On occasion, the statue might be buried and a false or "decoy" statue set up to fool the invaders. But if the invasion lasts for a long time, people may take the decoy to be the true deity, and the original statue is left forgotten.

Such statues are believed to be alive and have responses to the situation. Sometimes a statue was taken by the priest and sometimes it left on its own, floating through the air or animating its stone legs to run. The statue's running away was not viewed as cowardice on the statue's part, but rather as its faithfulness to its priest, caretaker, or village population—it did not want to be worshiped by foreigners. Sometimes the statue or rock could be convinced to return if the invaders promised to worship it and give large amounts of offerins, but usually it refused to return and roamed the forests and jungles until it found a suitable lake in which to rest.

The stone or statue may end up in the lake or ground in a variety of ways. Sometimes the stone is considered to be spontaneously alive, *svayambhu,* and the goddess has chosen to dwell there for her own reasons. She has been sleeping there for centuries, and she has suddenly awakened (or she has been waiting for the right person to finally call). Sometimes the statue is deliberately kept hidden in the water, especially to escape "torture by Muslim rulers."[4] A statue understood to be conscious would not enjoy having its nose or limbs knocked off, which often happened during Muslim attacks. This is locally understood by informants as deity torture. When the dream command comes to the sleeping person, the goddess has generally decided that it is time to move.

The person who has the dream, according to the origin stories, usually goes out and finds the rock or statue and arranges for its worship. Sometimes people ignore the dream, and then it recurs over and over until the person finally agrees to get the goddess. If the person is stubborn and will not get her, the goddess may curse him with all sorts of disasters until he feels compelled to get her rock or statue. After the rock is recognized as a goddess and given offerings, the dreams stop and the person can either be the special caretaker of the goddess or leave her to a priest. It is rare that she chooses to return to the lake or river, but it does occasionally happen.[5]

Goddess stones are occasionally said to change size, becoming larger or smaller over time. For instance, at Makardah village in Howrah, the stone of the goddess Makar Chandi was said to have gotten smaller over time. According to the story, the stone was once large enough to require the priest to climb a ladder to perform the daily worship. But when a priest came to resent the size of the stone and the extra work that was entailed for its worship, the goddess was upset, and sank into the earth and disappeared. The priest was then sorry for his resentment of the oversized goddess and begged her to return. She did so, but only in her current, diminished form.[6]

Stones and statues of gods and goddesses are loosely called "thakurs," or lords, by many village people. "*Āmār ṭhākur,*" my lord, does not generally refer to a deity in heaven, but rather to a deity on earth: the stone or statue in the house worship room (*ṭhākur ghar*). Thakurs have both upward and downward mobility. A rock or other object may be determined to be the dwelling place of a deity, placed in a house to be worshiped, and gain the respect of the family. If that family is blessed with luck, especially cures of disease, the family deity may start to be worshiped by the village. For instance, the Manasa stone of Tantipara was originally the household deity of a man named Nityananda Dhibar, and it gradually became known as the village deity.[7] The Uluichandi stone in the family house of one informant became popular as a living deity. It then was named as the village deity, and the informant's grandfather became its priest.[8]

As a village deity, the goddess stone may get its own temple and a full-time priest, who can accept offerings from the villagers and ritually offer them to her. People from other villages may come with offerings. It can get a reputation as a deity that is alive (*jagrata*), and its temple can become a place of pilgrimage. Sometimes it may be taken in procession to other villages, which keep an empty seat (*asana*) for its visit. The Manasa stone of Agar village in Birbhum visits many other villages in the area. Agar has three stones that represent the goddess Manasa; in large, medium, and small sizes (called Barama, Mejama, and Chotama). The small one is sent to other villages, or sometimes her place is taken by a clay or wooden horse (as her representative). When the clay horse is sent to Metela village, it is worshiped with devotion for a day on its small wooden throne with a red cloth, and then it is returned to its original shrine.[9] All castes worship the goddesses. In the town of Shibpur, there is joint worship of Kali by all villagers. Whenever a marriage party comes into the village, the couple must first bow down to the goddess, or trouble may occur. Once a couple did not bow to Kali and as soon as they passed her shrine, the handles of the wedding palanquin broke.[10]

In the case of goddess stones, if the temple is built where the stone was found, it may get the reputation of being a hidden Sati *pīṭha,* or place blessed by some body part of the goddess Sati. Or it may be a new Shakta site blessed by a goddess, not a historical one, blessed by the goddess' choice to dwell there. Relatively new *pīṭha*s have been claimed in West Bengal; probably the most famous of the newer ones are Tarapitha and Adyapitha.

There is also downward mobility among thakurs. When a stone or statue has not been doing its job, and the town or family has been unlucky, the statue may be understood as weak (however, if there are real disasters, the statue may also be viewed as strong but angry, and needing propitiation). If the statue is determined to be weak, or its worshipers leave and nobody else wishes to take on the responsibility of caring for it, it loses status. It may be consigned to the Ganges River or some other body of water, or it may be put into a temple of some other deity as an additional god or goddess, also cared for by the priest. Some temples become a sort of "old-age home" for thakurs, with unwanted gods donated along with money for their upkeep. There are sections for old goddess stones, *liṅga*s, Narayana stones, even small statues and photographs, in some temples. However, I have found the topic of getting rid of unwanted thakurs to be an embarrassing one for informants, perhaps comparable to getting rid of unwanted relatives. People are uncomfortable at leaving their grandfather's goddess in the spare room or sending her off to live on a temple's charity (such shame may show a bhakti or devotional element in this folk worship). In some cases, a deserted temple with a living deity may have the equivalent of "home health care"—a group or society may decide to hire a brahmin to visit the temple each day, to feed and care for the deity. This is because the ground on which the temple sits is sacred ground and it has been revealed that the deity wishes to stay in its own temple, on its own ground.

Another important aspect of folk Hinduism is the worship of goddesses in the form of old women. This is generally not seen in brahmanical Hinduism, where goddesses are portrayed as young and beautiful. In the folk tradition, there are many goddesses who are called Budi Ma or Buri Ma. In modern Bengali, *buḍī* means "old woman," but the folk meaning of the term is "ancestress," the woman who is old because she originated the group. She is not merely old, but ancient, and revered for her age and power. Some of these older goddesses are associated with trees (such as Vana Durga or Durga of the forests, and Budi Ma or Rupasi who dwells in the sheora tree). Nanimadhab Chaudhuri calls the Old Lady's worship "the cult of a tribal clan deity," and mentions Buri Thakurani, Burhia Mata, and Burhi Mai.[11] Hathi-dhara-Buri, the Old Lady who catches elephants with her hands, is said to have cleared the Midnapore jungle for her tribal followers by killing and chasing away the wild elephants (though now she has come to be brahmanized, and is also worshiped by Hindus). Sometimes the Old Lady is worshiped along with her consort, the Old Man, in the cult of Bura-Buri, especially in West Bengal, Bihar, and Assam. Chaudhuri notes three aspects as important in the worship of the Buri: the absence of any statue of the deity (she is worshiped as present in nature rather than in a particular form), the presence of outdoor shrines, and the *deyashi* or nonbrahmanical priest who leads her worship.[12] The Old Lady may be worshiped in a tree, in groups of plants with hibiscus and vermilion, or in a rock in the shrine.

In some instances various forms of the Old Lady are adopted into Hinduism. In this case her name changes (she becomes Vriddheshvari, the Aged Hindu Goddess), and the priest is usually a brahmin. A good description of this transformation was given by a land owner or zamindar:

> The cult prevails also among the higher castes among whom the Buri is known as Vrddhesvari. A Brahman officiates as priest. In the Brahmanical form of worship the goddess is meditated on as follows: "Goddess fair-complexioned, adorned with all kinds of ornaments, dressed in yellow garments, two-eyed, two-armed, beautiful and smiling, who always grants boons to her votaries." She is invoked as the nurse of the universe (*Jagatam dhatri*) and consort of Rudra (*Rudrakanta*). Goats and pigeons are sacrificed to her.[13]

We may note here that the aniconic folk goddess becomes a fair-skinned great goddess or Devi; the nature goddess is transformed into a distant deity of wealth and power, and consort of a Hindu god.

We see a similar phenomenon in the village of Asansol in Burdwan, with another Old Lady goddess, Ghaghrabudi. It is said by the people of the village that Ghaghrabudi dwelt within large pieces of stone under a tree on the bank of the river long before the village was built. She was found due to a flood in 1956, which uprooted the old tree and revealed the egg-shaped stones which were her home. According to the story, she had been the deity worshiped by a tribal community living in the forests, but as the tribal people moved out and brahmanical Hindu groups moved in, Ghaghrabudi decided to get worship from the Hindus. She appeared as an old woman wearing a *ghāghra* (a sort of skirt) before a depressed, suicidal brahmin named Kangal Chakravarti. She told him not to commit suicide, but instead to worship her in the form of the stones. He did so, worshiping her with the visualization of the goddess Chandika. As she was accepted by the Hindu community, her name was changed from Ghaghrabudi (the Old Woman or Ancestress in a skirt) to Ghaghrachandi (the tribal and folk goddess Chandi in a skirt) and later to Ghaghradevi (the Hindu great goddess in a skirt).[14] She is thus transformed from the tribal ancestor (*budī*) to the folk or village goddess (*caṇḍī*) and then to the brahmanical Hindu goddess (*devī*).

While the figures of older goddesses and ancestresses are found fairly frequently in folk religion, they are rare in brahmanical Hinduism. This may be a result of the different conceptions of power. The Old Woman of the Village or Jungle has the knowledge that she has gained through age and, like the creatures of nature, she shows both increase of knowledge and increase of years. The Hindu goddess may enter nature but her home is elsewhere, and she takes on the form that represents her power: the face of a sixteen-year-old girl and the breasts of a nursing mother. She thus combines the powers of eternal youth, beauty, and immortality with the symbols of nurturing and motherhood. Her power is not in her wisdom gained in years of survival, but comes innately. The major Bengali Hindu goddesses—Kali, Durga, Tara, Lakshmi, and Sarasvati—are generally shown as young and attractive. Even Kali, whose images in other regions of India are emaciated and ugly, is frequently shown as beautiful and voluptuous in West Bengal. It is the youth of the Hindu goddess that shows her power, as it is the age of the Adivasi goddess that shows her wisdom.

Chandi is a goddess who was partially adopted into the Hindu pantheon. Sometimes she is the patron deity of Adivasi or tribal people (especially in texts such as the *Chandi Mangal Kavya,* in which she is worshiped by a hunter and his wife), and sometimes she is a folk goddess and village housewife. Tribal hunters would carry her rock for luck in the field, though more often it would rest beneath a sacred tree or in a small hut.

As a Hindu goddess, Chandi is represented by a dark rounded rock or a piece of the remains of a bas relief, often daubed with vermilion. Sometimes the area of her face may have silver eyes or a mouth drawn on, and the rock is kept on a wooden throne. She may be accompanied by clay and terracotta horses and elephants, a pitcher or "god-pot," and a post for animal sacrifice. While in the folk style she may be worshiped by the village headman (*deyāsī*) or his wife (*deyāsinī*), in the brahmanical style she is worshiped by a brahmin priest. Both may involve processions with music and song. As she is further Hinduized, she may get a human body, carved out of clay or wood. For instance, the Chandi at Barisha shows Hindu tantric influence: she is carved in human form, and sits on a seat of human skulls (*pañcamuṇḍa āsana*) painted brown, pink, green, yellow, and blue. She has four arms, a garland of skulls, a crown and ornaments, and a red sari.[15]

Some rituals combine both styles, and the goddess may be worshiped by both a nonbrahmin priest (often the headman of the village) and a brahmin priest.

In the village of Khairadih near Bakreshwar, Mangal Chandi is usually kept in a mud temple and worshiped by a nonbrahmin priest of the weaver caste, but on her annual festival the nonbrahmin priest pays the expenses and a brahmin priest from another village is called to officiate. The shrine is cleaned and whitewashed and clay models of religious figures are exhibited. The goddess Manasa from Tantipara village is also brought for a visit. Mangal Chandi is placed by the brahmin priest on a wooden throne to circumambulate the village, and carried by members of the headman's family. The women of the headman's family lead the crowd, carrying the sacred pitcher, blowing conch shells and making the trilling sounds of ululation. The procession goes out to a sacred pipal tree, to perform the Gachbera ritual (encircling the tree). Eight women (of the headman's family) stand around the tree and then walk around it seven times. They unwind thread from a bamboo spool around the tree trunk. Then everybody else circles around the tree. There is music and the sound of conches. The procession then returns, and the deity is put back in her shrine.[16] Then the brahmin priest sits down to worship Mangal Chandi while the headman observes from a distance. The brahmin performs a fire sacrifice (*yajña*) and chants mantras in Sanskrit.[17] The goddess has not communicated whether she prefers a folk or orthodox Hindu style of worship.

Chandi may be associated either with good fortune or with disaster. She has many auspicious forms: Mangal Chandi, who is generally worshiped in a pitcher without an image, and brings good fortune; Jai Mangal Chandi, who gives children; Harish Mangal Chandi, who brings joy to the household; Sankat Mangal Chandi, who frees people from dangerous situations; Uday Mangal Chandi, who brings marriage, riches, and children; Natai Chandi, who is worshiped with joy and recovers lost treasures or relatives; and Rana Chandi, who brings victory in war.[18] However, she may also be a disease goddess, especially as Olai Chandi, the goddess of cholera. She has also been associated with plague, eye trouble, and cattle diseases. The goddesses reflect the pragmatic concerns of folk Hinduism, overcoming the fear involved in war, disease, and danger.

Chandi may also be invoked for both love magic and exorcism. Among the Savara people, Chandi is invoked by the shaman (*ojhā*) for the ritual of *dhuloparā,* the magical use of dust. The man who desires a woman gets the dust from her footsteps and brings it to the *ojhā,* who chants an incantation three times. The man then scatters the dust onto the woman, and she finds herself attracted to him. The *ojhā* chants:

> Dust, dust, dust, queen of dust
> O beloved one, listen to my words.
> I have taken the dust of the path with three fingers
> Very carefully, and with Mahamaya's blessings.
> I will take this dust in my fingers
> And I will scatter it on you
> When you are at the market, or elsewhere.

It will bind you to me, you will be mine forever.
By whose will? By the will of the goddess Kamakhya of Kanur.
By whose will? The goddess Chandi, the Hadi's daughter.
This dust will work quickly.[19]

In this invocation, the shaman and the man are linked—the chant by the *ojhā* is intended to benefit the man. He places a binding spell on the dust and it becomes magically powerful, so that the woman who receives the dust will fall in love with the man. The spell is believed to work because powerful goddesses are invoked to support the spell. These are Kamakhya, the Assamese tantric goddess associated with Kali, and Chandi, here described as the daughter of a low-caste person (thus sympathizing with lower-caste petitioners).

Chandi and Kali are also invoked as exorcism goddesses by the Savaras. The *ojhā* finds out who is possessing a person by looking into the water in a clay pitcher; it becomes a mirror where images of the supernatural are seen. After he sees the image, he performs a chant, listing the various possible entities who could be causing the trouble, and he exorcises the possessing entity in the names of Kali and Chandi.[20]

Such approaches are often called witchcraft by more brahmanical Hinduism. The role of witchcraft has changed in recent years, gaining a greater political focus, and accusations of witchcraft have come to be used for political scapegoats. I saw several articles following the theme of an article in the newspaper *Amrita Bazar Patrika,* entitled "Three Women Beaten for 'Witchcraft'." Two young tribal girls and their mother were severely beaten by supporters of the CPIM (Communist Party of India, Marxist) in Midnapore district, and were hospitalized. They were members of a rival political group, the DYFI, who had protested against local communist leaders demanding a percentage of their wages. After an unsuccessful attempt at rape, and ordered ostracism by the village, the local CPIM leader had the women beaten for witchcraft.[21] As is unfortunately the case in many countries of the world, accusations of religious misbehavior are often a cover for persecution with a more political and economic basis. This is an example of the negative way that politics and religion may interact. Most folk religion emphasizes worship and healing, rather than destructive action.

An example of living Bengali folk religion which contains brata rituals may be seen in the worship of the goddess Tushu.

2

The Folk Goddess Tushu, Her Festival, Songs, and Brata

One important aspect of Bengali folk religion is the prominence of festivals, or *melas*. Festivals are widespread in village Bengal and frequently involve music, songs, dance, worship of a natural object or sculptured image, and the sale of a variety of goods (food, garlands of flowers, worship items, plastic kitchen utensils). Some festivals are dedicated to gurus and saints, and there are usually pictures or posters with their images. During the bigger festivals, which are usually goddess *pūjās* (such as Durga Puja and Kali Puja) there will often be clay statues of the goddess available. These often portray the goddess in mythological roles and accompanied by associates and mounts (*vāhanas*).

One example of a festival in folk Hinduism to a local goddess is the Tushu festival, which is full of song and story. The major ritual of the festival is a procession involving symbols of the goddess (special rice balls), which are carried in paper chariots to the Suvarnarekha River and represent the return of the goddess Tushu to her husband, who lives beneath the waters. Tushu is compared to a daughter who visits her parents once a year and then returns to her home with her husband.

Tushu is an example of a goddess worshiped by both tribal and folk Hindu groups. Her major worship occurs during her yearly festival, and she is worshiped by people living in the western area of West Bengal, the eastern area of Bihar, and some portions of Orissa and Madhya Pradesh. According to anthropologists interviewed, it is "the most important village festival in West Bengal,"[1] and "along with the Bhadu festival, it is the largest village goddess festival in West Bengal."[2] The writer Kisalaya Thakur stated, "the most widespread and enthusiastic festival in the villages is Tushu,"[3] the anthropologist P. K. Bhowmick has called it "perhaps the most popular festival of the masses,"[4] and ethnomusicologist Suhrid K. Bhowmik has called it "the most popular folk festival of the southwest frontier of Greater Bengal."[5]

The festival is seasonal; it begins on the last day of the month of Agrahayan (about mid-December) and continues on through the whole month of Paush (until mid-January). It celebrates the end of harvest time, the relaxation after hard work, and it also ends the tribal year. It is celebrated by a variety of village and tribal peoples along the eastern part of the Jharkhand belt sometimes known as

Frontier Bengal, which includes Purulia, Bankura, and Midnapore districts. Tushu is an important goddess of the Jharkhand people, who have recently created their own state in India, called Jharkhand.

Many songs are sung every evening throughout the month of Paush to Tushu. Some people say that the songs are sung to awaken her, and others say that the songs are to please her so that the next year will be fruitful. Tushu is welcomed with song and dance during periods of rest and also during various household chores and other work. However, the climax of the festival is during the final three days of the month of Paush.

According to practitioners in Purulia, on the first of these three days, the protectress of seeds is worshiped, whose name is Chauri. She is associated with the goddess Chandi and also with Rohini, the woman who (according to Jharkhand tradition) discovered the first seed. She saw the seed on a hill slope, took soil with the seed, and grew the first cultivated plant. She is worshiped as a *buḍī* (ancestress) for this act, and called the *matrika* (mother) of seeds. On this day, all the rice on the farm should be brought to the family house. On the next day, small bundles of grain are made for the next year's crops, and put into the granary. This day is sacred to Bauri. She is associated with the clear sky, the movement of the stars and moon, and the cosmos as a whole. She is also goddess of animal behavior (as it is influenced by the heavens), and on this day she ritually dwells in the storage bin with the grain. On Bauri day, the goddess' chariot (*chaudel*) is purchased and two cowdung and rice balls put inside, representing the union of male and female qualities (cowdung is considered to be a good thing, for as fertilizer it encourages nature and growth). These balls have often been previously worshiped in house altars which are triangular wall niches, decorated with white rice paste. The balls are first placed in the niche and covered with flowers, and women sing before the altar. The unmarried women sing first, and later they are assisted by older women. This altar/niche is used for only one month of the year. In some areas, there is a Bauri *bāndhā,* or ritual of guarding seeds from the evil eye. Vermilion and rice powder are put on straw bins and baskets where rice paddy has been kept, and sometimes an old tree will also be offered rice powder and vermilion.[6]

The last day of the tribal year during the month of Paush is sacred to the goddess Tushu, and people celebrate fruit, flowering, and the harvest. It usually occurs about mid-January. One popular story says the Tushu festival originated in the thirteenth or fourteenth century, to commemorate a brave woman who defended the granary and fields against invaders. A recent Tushu song uses this imagery:

> Tushu has picked up a sickle in her hands
> And she is going to harvest that paddy
> Which is grown with blood.
> Landowners will come rushing up
> (But) Tushu has courageously made up her mind
> She holds the sickle with a firm grip.[7]

On the night before the new year is the awakening (*jāgaran*) of Tushu. Bonfires are lit from discarded rice husks, and young girls sing and dance around them. On the day of Tushu or Makar Sankranti, Tushu devotees gather in the morning for ritual baths in the river or ponds, and form processions which roam singing through the town.

At the 1994 Tushu festival in Tullin, people were awakened early in the morning by loudspeakers loudly playing taped Tushu songs, which continued through the day. Even the local Shiva temple had two loudspeakers. From early morning, women roamed in procession through the town, singing so that the year will be good, the goddess happy, and the crops healthy. Women in brightly colored saris and young girls in braids carried symbolic chariots over their heads made of bright paper and bamboo, called *chaudel*s (from *chāturdola* or four-sided chariot). These represented the chariot of Tushu. As the day went on, Tushu groups moved toward the main fairgrounds, along the banks of the Suvarnarekha river.

At the festival, one area was entirely taken up by men gambling in a variety of games. Winning at gambling at this time is believed by the players to bring a good year, and the men participated with great enthusiasm. Across the field, women carried dozens of Tushu chariots high overhead. Some were decorated on the outside with plastic dolls. Troops of women were singing, some accompanied by men playing flutes and heavy drums. There were about twenty to twenty-five thousand people at the festival, and informants estimated that the large celebration in that town has been occurring for at least 150 years. The language of the songs was neither Hindi nor Bengali, but regional languages such as Kurmali, which have no script (thus the songs were handed down by oral tradition). In recent years, some songs have been written down in Bengali script by Bengali observers, and most Tushu songs in print are written in the Bengali language. These songs are sung as the chariots are paraded through the fields and fairgrounds, and finally brought to the river's edge for their immersion. These chariots or "flower houses" are up to six feet tall and more or less rectangular, in the general shape of box kites, and their design appears to derive both from indigenous tribal images and Muslim shrine designs. Songs are sung at the time of immersion, wishing the goddess goodbye and inviting her back again next year.

In Purulia, there are no Tushu images or statues (*mūrti*s). Within the chariot, there is a small empty space, and within that is placed the sacred couple Tusha and Tushi, in the forms of two small balls of cowdung. Tushi's ball is topped with rice husks. Cowdung represents fertility, and it is the first fertilizer used in planting rice. Tusha is male, representing rain, dew, and fog, while Tushi represents the female earth. Both male and female are needed for reproduction. Together, the couple become Tushu—the goddess of fertility and its cycles. We have here the unusual situation of the union of a male and a female understood as one joint female—the deity Tushu. This is said by practitioners to represent the power of women, for Tushu is always a female name (thus showing how, in the couple, the woman dominates). This female dominance may be related to the fact that many of the families here do not follow the Indian dowry system, in which wedding money goes to the husband's family, but instead follow the tribal custom of bride price, in which the groom must offer payment for a wife to her parents.[8]

The themes of the older Tushu songs included the coming of Tushu, daily village life, prayers for happiness and prosperity, confiding of problems, household work of women, protests against male domination and relatives, lawsuits, property disputes, weddings, childbirth, love affairs, women's rituals, and local historical accounts of important events. In modern times, the rhythm and melody of the Tushu songs have been used in a variety of ways: for political songs and propaganda of political parties (the CPIM, Congress, and Jharkhand parties have all adopted these tunes), for commercial songs and secular love songs, as part of poetry and song competitions in Purulia schools (occurring only during the month of Paush), and it is a mark of high status to be a winner of the Tushu competition. Songs also protest against unethical business practices, corruption, and immorality.

Many Tushu songs are confessional in nature. Some songs deal with daily and ritual anxieties—family difficulties, lack of food, inability to celebrate properly because of poverty. Sometimes there is muted criticism: rather than saying that a local mother does not care for her children properly, the song might say that Yashoda is letting the baby Krishna play in the dirt, and now he must be washed because he is covered with mud. Or instead of saying that a husband stays out all night drinking with his friends, the singer might refer to Sita waiting for Rama to return, criticizing Rama for leaving her to pine away.

There are three major tunes for Tushu songs, and during the month of Paush a wide variety of songs are sung following them. The songs follow the mainstream Hindu notion of *bhāvas*—different religious roles through which the goddess is understood. The major roles appear to be Tushu viewed as mother or goddess, as child, as friend, as beloved, and as protector. These differ from the five traditional Vaishnava *bhāvas* in including the role of protector instead of *śānta* or peaceful mood, and mother/goddess instead of lord and master. The god as son becomes the goddess as daughter. However, the Tushu songs do not include the traditional Shakta *bhāva* of blame, seen in the poetry of mainstream Hindu writers who worship the goddess.[9] Tushu has the roles of mother and daughter seen in Shakta devotional songs, but the child does not complain about the mother's behavior. There is certainly protest, but it is against worldly events rather than against the goddess and her behavior. There are also secular songs that follow the Tushu tunes, including local oral histories, love songs, and commercial songs.

Sometimes a song may combine *bhāvas*, as this song describes Tushu as both mother and daughter:

Tushu is our goddess (*debī*)
Tushu is our protector
But she is also our daughter
And we worship her.

> This year, we had a drought
> So our worship of Tushu is not luxurious.
> But next year, Tushu, by your grace
> Our prayers will be answered
> And our crops will be lush.
> Then we can worship you
> With joy and happiness and feasting.[10]

As a goddess, she is sometimes understood to be a local personification of agricultural fertility, and sometimes a goddess of the water that fertilizes the land. In this song Tushu is a river goddess, returning to her husband under the river. This song is sung when he chariot is immersed in the river at the end of the festival:

> The water splashes and flashes (on the stones).
> O Tushu, who is there beneath the sparkling stones?
> Is he related to you?
> O, my mother and father are both there
> And my man is beneath the stones.
> The sound of the river water is like rhythmic music.
> O my friend, please tell me,
> Where are you going?[11]

The process of immersion may have been taken from the Hindu goddess festivals, in which the statues are immersed at the end of the *pūjā*s. Here immersion is not final, for a nature goddess can always dwell invisibly on the earth:

> O Ma Tushu, we are your daughters,
> So why don't you speak to us?
> Is it because today is the immersion?
> O Ma Tushu, please don't be angry.
> Don't separate yourself from us.
> Next year we'll carry you again.
> This is not really a separation.
> You are (still) in the paddy field
> With us.[12]

In another song, Tushu is called the goddess of the universe, *jāgaṭ devī*:

> O Tushu, who has thrown dust
> On your golden body?
> O my Tushu, you are the goddess of the universe.
> You are so beautiful.
> And today, the men are grinding rice for you.[13]

17

In such songs, we see the influence of Hindu theology and Sanskrit terminology: the phrase *jāgat devī* is not a folk term. However, Tushu is primarily a local goddess, and vows and promises are made to her during her month of worship (these vows are called *mānat*):

> O Tushu, this year we had a drought.
> I shall call you next year.
> The males have left (for work)
> And they have not yet returned.
> I promise you, O Tushu,
> If my eldest brother is blessed with a son
> Then I shall expand our granary
> And make it a two-storied building.[14]

Songs about Tushu in the role of daughter echo the annual visit of the actual daughter from the husband's house for three days each year. In those areas where the daughter goes to live in the husband's family household (following the Hindu style of patrilocal marriage), her visits back to her natal family are highly valued and celebrated. As at Durga Puja in more urban and Hindu areas, the family welcomes the daughter with happiness. Songs about this event are often sung while the women do household chores:

> Our beloved Tushu, you have come back home.
> We will worship you.
> The time of relaxation after harvesting has begun
> And we will happily go singing.[15]

The songs in the daughter-*bhāva* often focus on the son-in-law: they tend to either praise him as a way of making him extend his visit (and thus the daughter also gets to stay longer), or say that the son-in-law is not treating his new wife well enough and she should stay with her parents. Here is an example of the first theme:

> O Tushu, what happened to our son-in-law?
> We are sending letters and also a horse,
> Yet still he doesn't come.
> We welcome him warmly
> With hospitality and graciousness,
> But still he stays for only three days.
> O son-in-law, stay for more than three days
> And we'll give you many kinds of food.[16]

The family is close to the daughter and does not want her to leave for the home of the in-laws:

When my Tushu must go,
My eyes fill with tears.
Tushu, you have lived with us for thirty days
And now you say you won't leave your mother,
But that isn't true:
You are going away.
On Paush Sankranti (day), the son-in-law will come
And he will take you away.
But we will quarrel with him.
We will not let him take you.
We will not give you to him, or even admit that he is the son-in-law.
We will fight with him (for you).[17]

Sometimes Tushu is an older daughter, and the songs have advice from her mother:

O Tushu, please do not cry
Obey your husband Dugga.
My son-in-law is a good man
And he surely loves you!
Here in the house of your father, a farmer,
Please come visit during the Paush festival.
And Tushu, submit to your husband Dugga.[18]

Tushu as a friend may sympathize with problems, especially those which may be difficult to discuss with others in the village. Many women fear to publicize such situations as wife beating and hostile mates, but these can be sung about in Tushu songs. In this song, the singer not only admits problems in her marriage, but has already thought of an alternative (a local cowherd):

Come, Tushu, come, we shall go to the bridge
At the crossing of the Sarada (river).
We shall bathe in the waters
And dry our hair in the sun.
I have endured once being beaten, and then I have stood it again,
But I will not allow it more than three times.
O my husband's sister, go and say
That I won't do the housework anymore.
A cow has given birth to a calf by the riverside
And its name is laughter (Hashi).
I shall buy the cowherd some fruit
With my brass ring.[19]

Sometimes the problem of beatings is due to the mother-in-law rather than the husband, as this woman states (though she sounds equally angry at her own parents for getting her into this situation):

> There is spinach[20] on the top of the thatched roof,
> And I shall enjoy eating it.
> I shall no longer go to the house of my in-laws,
> For my mother-in-law will beat me.
> I have tolerated one blow from her fist, and even two,
> But the third blow I shall not tolerate.
> Had my parents come to visit just once
> I would not have looked at them.[21]

In areas that have less bride-price and more Hindu influence of arranged marriage and dowry, the parents may choose an inappropriate husband for the daughter. The husband may be old, but the girl-wife has no choice:

> My uncle, you took a hundred rupees
> And gave it to my ancient husband.
> When I walk with my husband in the town of Ranigunj,
> People ask me how I am related
> To this old man.
> I feel terribly embarrassed.
> He is as old as my grandfather.[22]

Some Tushu songs are ostensibly sung to the goddess, but they are really intended for others:

> I shall take a pot of oil and a towel
> And go to bathe in Mallik's pond.
> O sweetheart, you are cruel and a thief.
> You gave me hope, but now
> You are living in another's house.[23]

Tushu may help her devotees in activities that are not traditionally religious ones. This song is sung by a married woman to her lover:

> In the town of Puruliya (in Purulia district),
> The women are the shopkeepers.
> O Tushu, I pray to you,
> In my next birth, please make me a shopkeeper
> So that I can at least sell something good, with a smile
> To my beloved.[24]

As a friend, Tushu may also be given advice by the neighborhood women about undesirable occupations. As in many countries, teachers are underpaid here:

> Tushu is a schoolteacher.
> She can't get a full meal
> And torn rags cover her body!
> Because you are educated,
> Lamentation is your fate!. . .
> O Tushu, I beg you,
> Don't become a teacher.
> While you are growing up,
> Don't starve yourself to death.
> Do not hold a pen in your delicate hands.
> Please do not be a teacher.[25]

Some songs speak of lost love:

> Oh dark boy, you have made me love you.
> You made me weep here along the road.
> You hold the moon of heaven in your hands.[26]

Often these songs use the meter and melody of Tushu songs, but not the name of the goddess:

> You have tormented me by loving me.
> I cannot remove you from my mind.
> I loved you silently, but what made you change today?
> I won't look at your face.
> You do not understand the secret of love.
> I had to talk to you, and gave excuses so that I could look at you,
> But now you are so indifferent, you have forgotten everything.
> I do not want to hear your voice, I do not like what you have become.
> I want to sacrifice my life.
> My reputation is lost because of you.
> What will happen to me in the future?
> I can only spend the rest of my life
> Thinking of the end.[27]

Many of the songs are quite outspoken, for a country often said to lack romantic love:

> O my beloved friend, you are [as close as] the pupil of my eye.
> I go mad when I don't see you.

I hinted to you with a sideways look.
I am bewildered because you have gone.
This flower has budded and bloomed
But it has not yet gained fragrance and taste.
I want to become the nectar of flowers
You can be the honeybee.[28]

Often metaphors from nature are used:

The hunter of love sits tight
And aims his gun at the target,
But then it is he who feels the pain,
Like a deer pierced by an arrow.
The parrot and the maynah bird
Proclaim the glory of Radha and Krishna,
But Lord Vishnu hears Tushu's songs
And he is bound in a knot of love.[29]

During the month of Paush, there are mock competitions associated with Tushu processions, in which groups of males and females talk about the superiority of their own group and Tushu chariot or statue, while insulting that of the other group. Group leaders fight over precedence in walking down the road, or crossing a stream.

In the village rivalries, themes of fertility often emerge. There is both conflict and flirtation between the groups of young men and women. There may be teasing and songs of attempted seduction and rebuff:

Men: Tomato juice is dripping.
You are just like that,
But you can't see your own (menstrual) juices.
Women: So what? They are not meant for you.
Men: Then who are they for?
Women: Not for you.
You'll have to be reborn in order to get me.[30]

In this case, menstruation implies ripeness and availability (at least to the men). Charges and countercharges are sung. During the festival, different groups make their own houses and images of Tushu, and these are carried in procession. Often one Tushu is claimed to be more attractive or powerful than another:

My Tushu has eaten *pān* (betel-leaf)
And looks very beautiful.
The *pān* of your Tushu has no taste

And your Tushu has made love with
A tasteless man.
My Tushu has put on a fine necklace
And it glitters about her neck.
The necklace of your Tushu is full of thorns
And the lover of your Tushu is blind.[31]

The Tushus are usually carried by the women, and the men accompany them with drums and flutes. There are songs and dances on the streets, and mock fights:

My Tushu fries *muṛi* (puffed rice) and her bangles glitter.
Your Tushu is like a beggar, she wants everything,
And she spreads out her *ănchal* (the end of a sari)
So that my Tushu will give her the puffed rice.[32]

Tushu is also the protector and defender of the village people. When they are mistreated, they turn to her for inspiration and protection.

O Ma Tushu
By your grace we had a golden harvest
And we are preparing cakes
In your honor.
Please tell us how
To teach those moneylenders a lesson.
O Tushu, now you must become our leader
In raising our protest
Against the moneylenders.[33]

She defends the underclass against its enemies:

Tushu will no longer stand the tyranny of the rich.
People working hard in the fields
Do not get enough to eat,
And they suffer beatings without resisting.
My Tushu will not stand this any longer.[34]

In the modern situation, there are protests against dams, poor working conditions, multinational corporations, and prejudice. In the following song, Tushu is equated with the goddess Rankini Devi, who is both the royal lineage goddess of the Raj states of Dhalbhum and Jamboni (and thus the guardian deity of the princely states) and also a goddess of the Santal tribal people. She is associated with human sacrifice at the Rankini Mahula village temple in Birbhum, but she is also the protector of her people:

Jaya Ma Rankini, we worship at your feet.
O Mother, goddess of illusion (*māyāvinī*),
Compassionate and merciful,
This world is full of *māyā*.
But what has happened to our country?
The forests have been cut down
And towns have emerged,
And with them, the Tata Steel Company.
Jaya Ma Rankini, we worship at your feet.
So many people are working, mostly Bengalis,
As doctors, clerks, and mechanics
In the company.
And we are outside, we are just coolies.[35]
O Ma Rankini
O Ma Tushu
Please protect us.[36]

Tushu is called upon to protect India from Chinese aggressors, to pacify warring factions, and to comment on the end of the world (in which children disobey their parents, high-caste boys sleep with low-caste girls, people marry without their parents' consent, people stop working and depend on winning the lottery, and men wear sunglasses and wristwatches). She is like a family member or friend, but she also has powers of protection and nurturing.

Tushu's roles are slightly different among the tribal Oraon people. Here we see two major interpretations of Tushu. In one, she is equated with the Hindu goddess Lakshmi and worshiped by Hindu-style *pūjā* ritual. These songs glorify Tushu as beautiful and merciful and invoke other Hindu goddesses, such as Sarasvati. The tribal shaman, or *ojhā,* performs the Hindu *ārati* ceremony to Tushu as Lakshmi, the Hindu goddess of fortune and fertility. He offers flowers, sweets, fire, and incense to her, and the women of the village make their offerings after him and sing songs associated with fields and fruit. At the end of the festival, the women bid farewell to Tushu, who is said to be returning to the house of her in-laws. They sing to ease the pain of her leaving the parental home and moving to the husband's home:

When you go to your in-law's house,
Do not weep, dear.
Sarasvati will go with you,
As well as her four maidens, dear.[37]

In the other role, she is more human than divine, a personification of the village wife, and the songs teach her to act correctly:

Tushu, perform the evening rituals
Dear, you are a good housewife.
Do the evening rituals, Tushu,
Then you can go out.[38]

Some songs describe day-to-day life and the difficulties involved:

I made a fence around the house and built the walls,
But I couldn't fix the door.
The roof was damaged, and water poured through
Soaking Tushu's bed.[39]

Poverty and bad weather are major problems:

The storms came, the rains came,
Mango skins are floating on the flood waters.
Tushu is starving
And she eats the mango skins.[40]

Usually, Tushu is a sympathetic figure. However, sometimes she is portrayed as a disobedient child and her behavior, especially laziness, is criticized:

O, you bad, dark girl,
I would not feed you, even with old rice!
I will lock you in the cooking house
And you will get sick.
But after a strong kick in the rump
Your "disease" will disappear![41]

When she is portrayed as a young girl, her behavior with the boys in the neighborhood may be unacceptable:

O, you bad girl
You have made (the boys) fall in love with you.
Your lover is (like) the moon in heaven
But you have made him cry in the street.[42]

Further songs detail her problems as a new wife and as a married woman. She is warned to follow local traditions and customs and treat her children well. Such songs can serve to instruct new wives in proper behavior.

Oraons allow songs that have a less reverent image of the goddess Tushu—for instance, several of their songs refer to her as *kālo chhurī*, a loose, dark woman or "dirty girl" as Das and Raha translate it. She can represent human women in many situations. This approach would be quite sacrilegious for the Mahatos of Purulia, for Tushu there is more goddess and less woman—indeed, she is the major Jharkhand (regional) goddess. For the Oraons, however, she represents the tribal girls who are ignorant of proper womanly behavior, who ignore traditional mores and often suffer as a result. Her range of symbolism differs between one group and another. The respected goddess of one tribal group is the low-status woman of another.

The Tushu festival tradition is now in jeopardy. At the 1994 Tushu mela, the songs were whispered by the women—they did not wish to be heard singing. This is because of the politicization of the songs—people might think that they were singing songs of the various political parties rather than their own songs. The women were afraid to be heard. What is sometimes called "cultural silence" was very clear here. Having gained a voice with which to speak out against the problems of social life, they found that voice taken away by those who wished to speak out only about political groups. Ironically, the greatest fear seemed to be of the Communist Party of India, Marxist (CPIM), whose platform emphasizes that it is the voice of the people.

There was also a growing specialization with which to contend. People were awakened early in the morning by loudspeakers playing Tushu music sung by professionals, and now tapes are also available by professional singers. Individual, spontaneous voices seem unskilled by comparison. Thus we see a folk tradition rebelling against the mainstream co-opted by professionals, a spontaneous art form in which people become ashamed of their spontaneity.

One response to their difficult political and economic situation has been work toward the creation of a new state in India. In the words of Pashupati Mahato, an activist for the creation of the new state of Jharkhand:

> Tushu songs are a mirror of the culture, showing the concerns of the people, the influence of *bhakti* (devotion), the alienation from political rulers. The festival commemorates when the tribals adopted agriculture, and developed their own civilization. The first seed was discovered by a woman, and Tushu celebrates its flowering and fruit. It celebrates the self-expression of women, who become fierce and mad to defend the fields; women are protectresses, as is the goddess. These Tushu songs are their protests, and the protests of all *mulvasis* (root or original people), who have lost their cultural strength, and are forced to imitate the dominant cultural values.[43]

The state of Jharkhand was recently created by the Indian government, primarily for low-caste Hindu and tribal people, from land in the states of West Bengal, Bihar, Orissa, and Madhya Pradesh. It is the hope of its inhabitants that local forms of religion will be able to be practiced freely there.[44] There is also hope that

26

their language and culture will undergo a renaissance, and that they will not be taken advantage of economically and politically.

In Hindu folk religion, the most well-known form of worship for the goddess Tushu is her festival. However, Tushu is also worshiped in a more personal way, by means of a brata ritual. The Tushu brata involves a variety of actions and chants, but no story (*kathā*). The brata emphasizes good fortune, which the performer will gain by following the rituals.

There are several possible derivations for the name Tushu. It may be derived from the term for chaff (*tuṣ*), or from the constellation (*nakṣatra*) of the star Tiṣya, during which the festival takes place.[45] It may also come from the Santali word *tuṣu,* meaning bud or leaf (thus being a symbol of youth and beauty), or from the Bengali words *toṣ* or *toṣe,* meaning fresh and lively.[46] Many scholars believe that the Tushu festival is an ancient one and originates with the brata of Tus-Toṣali. As Yajnisvara Chaudhuri states,

> The worship of Tusu began with the tribal rites associated with the harvest deity, and the Tus-Tosali brata is the changed and abridged form of this worship of Tusu.[47]

A *brata* (or *vrata*, in Sanskritic form) involves a vow taken by Hindu men or women, usually for the purpose of bringing blessings to the family. All women—married, unmarried, and widowed—can participate in the brata rituals of Tushu, from the last day of the month of Agrahayan to the last day of Paush. The brata to Tushu is called the Tus-Tosali brata. It is performed differently in various regions of West Bengal.

In Burdwan (Bardhaman), to perform the Tushu brata, the women prepare twenty-one balls of mixed cowdung and rice chaff, which are kept on earthen plates. Over them are placed *asvattha* tree leaves and eggplant leaves. Then clay statues of an old man and woman are made. These are said to represent the the ancestors or first parents of the village people. Tushu here is represented by a divine couple and incorporates both male and female imagery. The term used for female ancestor is *buḍī,* or "old woman" in modern Bengali, and the term for male ancestor is *buḍā,* or "old man." These are worshiped early each morning with mustard flowers.

In some villages (especially those having had strong Hindu influence), the old couple is no longer worshiped and an image of the goddess Lakshmi has taken their place. Worship is performed for a month, and at the end of this time the plates and their contents are thrown into the water.[48]

Alternatively, the woman following the Tushu brata (the *bratinī*) takes her morning bath, and then makes 144 small mounds of cowdung and stores them atop eggplant leaves on a large clay plate. Each mound has five pieces of *dūrbā* grass and some vermilion on top. Then the woman scatters husks from rice and powdered rice on the mounds and collects flowers of mustard, kidney-bean, and radish, placing these on the plate. The *bratini* then walks through the rice fields with other woman performing the same ritual, and they sing songs to the goddess Tushu. These songs emphasize the blessings the women will attain from following the ritual: they will gain wealth, rice, cows which give much milk, and a happy household (capable sons, famous sons-in-law, well-behaved daughters, and a husband with a long life). On the last day of the month, the women wake early and walk to a river or pond with the plates and their ingredients, carrying a lamp. As the sun rises they throw the plates into the water, and then bathe. While bathing they worship Tushu (also called Toshla Devi) and the sun, and when they leave the water they recite stanzas worshiping the sun. In some cases, the cowdung mounds are thrown by the *bratini* onto her family's fice fields, to make them more fertile.[49]

The Tus-Tosali brata asks for specific gains in its ritual chant, especially wealth and a happy family.[50] The brata instructions say that married women who observe this brata will grant happiness to both their own ancestors and the ancestors of their in-laws. A song from the brata:

> O Tusali rai (Radhika)[51]
> O Tusali mai (mother)
> What boons shall I get after worshiping you?
> I want a father who is like a god and a guru,
> I want a mother (who swims) in an ocean of wealth,
> I want a husband who is lord of the country,
> I want a son-in-law who shines in the assembly,
> I want a brother who is a scholar in the king's court,
> I want a son who brightens the community.
> Let the *sindūr*[52] on my part blaze!
> Let my iron bracelet sparkle!
> Let my (many) clothes fly on the line!
> Let the kitchen utensils glitter!
> O, *sindūr* on my part, and rice in the granary.
> This young woman prays for these boons.[53]

Such bratas are often performed by women to help and bless their families. In West Bengal, their major usage is to create virtuous daughters and wives.

3

What Is a Brata?

While travelling in rural areas of India, an observer may see young village girls performing bratas. They stand with folded hands before the older women of the village, their mothers and grandmothers and neighbors, and listen to the stories of gods and goddesses. The girls learn to create miniature worlds, small forests and lakes and fields, and to care for and nurture them. They learn that the deities are merciful toward those who are willing to make sacrifices, and they fast from water or hot food for a day, or go for a day without a bath or a change of clothes. The old and young learn to appreciate each other, because there are bratas which revere both young girls and old women, and the generations are linked together through telling stories and performing rituals.

What is a brata? A brata is a vow or promise, usually to a deity, associated with a ritual practice. It is generally performed in order to gain some goal—a husband, a happy family with many sons, wealth, a job, or recovery from disease or disaster. In many brata stories, village women or goddesses save families from danger or rescue the souls of their selfish and uncharitable dead husbands from a hellish afterlife. While religious elements of austerity and purity often appear, the goal of the brata is not to detach the performer from the physical world, bringing him or her closer to *Brahman* or Ultimate Reality (or even the heaven world of a worshiped deity), but rather to gain blessings and a desired worldly outcome. There are folk bratas handed down by oral tradition and performed by village women, which ask various local deities for blessings, and there are more formal bratas, which are based on classical, brahmanical Indian religious literature, the Vedas and puranas and dharmashastras. While folk bratas are performed by women of all ages, more brahmanical bratas may be performed by both men and women (though rarely by unmarried men).[1] And there are many bratas in between, mixing elements of both.

There has been much useful research on bratas, both textual and anthropological. Susan Wadley and Laxmi Tewari have done research on folk brata stories from Uttar Pradesh, and there has been work on women's story-telling traditions in that area by Gloria Raheja and Ann Gold. The work of Mary McGee and Anne Pearson are both particularly important for the topic.

In her dissertation on bratas, *Feasting and Fasting: The Vrata Tradition and Its Significance for Hindu Women,* Mary McGee examines the Sanskrit traditional texts, the puranas, nibandhas, and dharmashastras, for their understanding of bratas. She notes that women see the rites as obligatory to dharma rather than optional, and that they contribute to *saubhāgya,* "the state of marital felicity," and promote auspiciousness. She calls bratas "the primary vehicle available to women for the recognized pursuit of religious duties and aims," and she has surveyed the meanings of the term "vrata" (brata) in Vedic literature: as command, religious duty, devotion to a particular deity, proper behavior, and religious commitment; and she notes the debates on the Sanskrit origins of the term.[2] According to P. V. Kane, the term "vrata" comes from the tracks or routes that stars and planets trace in the heavens. They are "commands or ordinances, religious or moral practices, or worship and vows,"[3] as well as "religious practices or modes of sacred worship."[4] They are associated with the cosmic order and with dharma, as fixed principles which were laid down by the gods. The term "vrata" is found in the *Rig Veda,* in dharmashastra texts (especially the nibandhas), and in the puranas and histories. The medieval puranas emphasized the access of all people to brata rituals.[5] Bratas were simpler, easier, and less expensive than Vedic sacrifices, and they did not always require a priest. Descriptions are found throughout the puranas, and P. V. Kane's *History of Dharmasastra* estimates that 25,000 verses in the puranas deal with bratas.

Anne Mackenzie Pearson's book *Because It Gives Me Peace of Mind: Ritual Fasts in the Religious Lives of Hindu Women*[6] explores the sociology of bratas in the Banaras area, observing women of urban Banaras and their practice of bratas. She shows the wide variety of motivations that cause women to perform these rituals, and observes how bratas are complex phenomena, with values of both auspiciousness and purity, care for others, and desire for improving individual lives, helping with problems and expressing personal faith. She notes that female practitioners in Banaras understand the bratas as duty, as resolve, as ethical action, and as spiritual practice, or *sādhanā,* as well as family rituals and devotional practices.

Susan Wadley, an anthropologist working in a village near Delhi in Uttar Pradesh, notes that bratas are a part of women's obligations or *strīdharma* in mainstream Hinduism and an important aspect of being a perfect wife. It gives women "active control of events," from helping out in the family to saving the husband or brother from death.[7] She emphasizes the importance of transmission of rites and kinship. Gloria Raheja and Ann Gold, also working in Uttar Pradesh, emphasize women's voices as self-affirming, having their own notions of the good life and trying to attain them. They disagree with the popular assumption that women have fully accepted the ideas of female subordination often seen in Hindu culture.[8] Laxmi Tewari has a collection of fifty-five bratas from Uttar Pradesh, and has many details of oral history.[9]

Bratas are usually optional rituals, performed for special blessings from the Hindu deities. The earlier Vedic and dharmashastra texts describing bratas had a greater priestly focus, and the later puranas had a lesser focus on priests and brahmanical ritual. However, we could say that the interaction here between the "great and little traditions" goes both ways: the classical literature shows less priestly fo-

cus over time, while the folk brata rituals, primarily transmitted through oral tradition, later start to emphasize gifts to brahmins.

Brata means "the taking of a vow," and it involves undergoing certain practices in order to achieve a desired aim. It usually involves fasting, following the
moral and ritual lessons of a story (*kathā*), creating artistic diagrams (*ālpanā*), and
reciting special verses or mantras. There are a wide variety of bratas, and today
there are many collections of bratas in book form published in West Bengal.[10]
Bratas may be performed at morning, evening, or night, every day for a month, or
on particular days of the year, or for several years in succession. Locales may vary
widely: they may be performed on river banks, under trees, outside in courtyards,
or inside one's house. They tend to be household rather than temple oriented,
though occasionally some girls go to temple priests.[11] Performers usually abstain
from food, sexuality, alcohol, and gambling—pleasure of any sort. Some bratas
forbid only certain types of food or drink.

A folk brata may be learned from a mother or grandmother, a more distant
female relative, or an older female neighbor. Bratas and their associated artistic diagrams (*ālpanā*) have also been occasional subjects of college courses—for instance,
at Vishvabharati University's Kalabhavana school in Shantiniketan, West Bengal.

The brata is understood by means of a story (the *brata kathā*) that explains
the history of the brata and the reasons for performing it. Whether the ritual as
sociated involves total fasting, avoiding certain foods or activities, or creating symbolic images, the story is the centerpiece of the event. Many of the brata stories involve goddesses. A frequent theme is the accidental or deliberate offending of the
goddess, who then comes down to take her revenge upon the offender. The story
then shows how she is pacified and returns to a state of harmony with her devotees. As the tension is resolved in the story, so some conflict or problem may also
be resolved in the daily lives of the women who perform the bratas. Brata stories
show examples of atoning for sins and ending household arguments, and show
that optimism and generosity are possible even in difficult situations.

It is traditionally the case that married women act as instructors, teaching
girls from the age of five years onward about the brata rituals. At that age, the girl
is taught to pluck flowers, dig pits for those bratas that require them, draw *ālpanā*
pictures on the floor or entrance to the house, model small statues, and learn
mantras. Each brata has its own alpana image—drawn with new clay whitened
with powdered rice dissolved in water. Alpana diagrams give ritual protection
from danger and/or fertility, and may be accompanied by pictures that represent
the desired goal or object. Some bratas include history—for instance, the Se-
jutibrata alpana represents the defeat of the Dom (a low-caste lineage) rulers by
invaders. There are also royal alpana, for the stability of the government, with the
"seat of God" diagram drawn on a ceremonial wooden stool.

The term *ālpanā* or *ālipanā* comes from a Sanskrit word (*ālimpanā*), whose
root "lip" here means "to plaster (with the fingers).[12] In other areas of India, they
are called *rangolī, kolam,* and other terms. Alpana designs are also used for im-

portant ritual occasions like marriage, the sacred thread ceremony (an initiation rite for religious adulthood), the child's first rice eating, and certain offerings to the ancestors. After the designs are painted (often including images of vines, trees, flowers, animals, stars and planets, people, footprints, or desired objects), a pot or pitcher made of clay or copper (the *mangal-ghaṭ*) is placed in the center of the alpana, with a twig placed in it. This pot represents the presence of the deity.

According to Tapan Mohan Chatterji in his book *Alpona,* these alpanas attained their highest development in Bengal,[13] and were used for all important religious and social ceremonies. The designs were drawn on the courtyard or floor of a house, and sometimes on low wooden stools or the upper side of winnowing fans (used for separating grain from chaff). Occasionally, they were seen on the outer surface of ritual pitchers.

Alpana designs are usually made of rice paste mixed with water and drawn by the woman, who dips the fingers of her right hand into the white paste. It is a more detailed sort of finger painting, and her hands are used as brushes for the design. The artist begins in the center of the design and works outward, adding decorative elements. Each alpana has a set of ritual forms required by the brata, but decorative additions may be added according to the artist's taste. While most alpanas are drawn in white rice paste, some include colored designs, with color either from pressed plants growing in the area or from the dust of powdered charcoal or brick.

According to Chatterji, girls would traditionally start learning how to draw alpana at six and seven years of age, and by thirteen or fourteen would become skilled.[14] He states that the designs are always done by women and never by men. However, in modern Calcutta such traditions may be ignored as commercial elements enter in—I saw men who were professional shrine makers making alpanas for the shrines (*pāṇḍāl*s) during the 1993 celebration of Durga Puja. These also involved the use of bright colors.

Bratas have continued in traditional style for centuries. They were already an ancient tradition when Shib Chunder Bose wrote his *Hindoos As They Are* in 1881, in which he describes the brata rituals of the time. He stated that when the girl is five years old, she is initiated by an older woman into the brata rituals, to assure a good husband and happiness. She might begin with a Shiva Puja brata, following the example of the goddess Durga (for Shiva is regarded as a model husband in many brata stories, more faithful than the flirtatious god Krishna). She makes a clay image, washes and sprinkles it with water, and prays while visualizing the form of the goddess. She then performs the brata of Hari with flowers and sandal paste and worships ten images of people and saints, and paints alpana designs on the floor. For those older forms of Hinduism that allowed polygamy, most notably in the medieval period, the girl might practice curses against her potential rival co-wife (*satin*), uttering such statements as, "May Sateen become a slave..."[15]

We see another early description of a brata in Joguth Chunder Gangooly's book from 1860, *Life and Religion of the Hindoos, with a Sketch of My Life and Ex-*

perience. In this case, it is a brata to Yama (lord of karma and the afterlife), here called Jom. Yama is also equated by the author with the Roman god Pluto (thus showing the author's British education):

> "Jom Pooker" (Pluto's Tank) is a vat dug in the earth, nearly three feet square and one foot deep; some waterlilies are planted in it, small alligators and sharks made of earth are put in also; the images of Pluto are placed on the four corners of the tank. Before breakfast the young girl comes to worship the tank with flowers. Sitting by it she pours a little water into the tank, then puts flowers on the head[s] of the Plutos, offering prayers in poetry. Here is the translation: "I worship this tank of Pluto. As a reward, I will feed on cream-cakes on plates of gold, and wear *shun-kho* forever." In the afternoon is the worship of Sha jooty [Sejuti]. There is a large collection of drawings on the floor. . . . The accompanying plate contains Sha jooty, with the pictures as drawn by the Hindoo girl. She uses prayers in rhyme, and I will translate one which she offers to Shiba [Shiva]: "O god Shiba, grant that I may not fall into the hands of a dunce."[16]

The goal of this brata was wealth and a good husband. At a time when arranged marriages were prevalent and young women had little say about who they would marry, using bratas in an effort to avoid being married to a dunce was not an entirely unreasonable act.

Brata rituals are associated with stories known as *bratakathās*, and these stories may be remembered and told to the younger generation by the older, or read from texts. McGee, who worked largely on shastric bratas of classical Hinduism, states that the brata stories do not give the origins of the rituals:

> There is a mistaken notion that *vrata* stories tell of the origin of a particular votive observance. Instead one gets the impression from most *vrata* stories that the observance had been around for quite a while, and what we have revealed to us in the story is but one particular episode of the observance of this *vrata* in the life of one particular person or family. . . . Even in the stories that tell of the performance of a *vrata* by a goddess and present this performance as the model on which human performances should be based, as happens in several stories in which Siva tells Parvati about a *vrata* she had performed earlier, the goddess is not viewed as having invented the *vrata,* but simply as having taken up its performance, usually on the advice of a sage who informed her of its availability. Thus the *vrata* stories always take up their narrative in the middle of the continuing history of the *vrata.*[17]

This sense of ancient tradition is often seen in the bratas that emphasize the classical Hindu religion and literature. However, if we look at the more regional Bengali folk bratas, it is clear that many of them do speak of the origin of the brata, usually in the interaction of a human woman and a goddess. The goddess helps the woman out of a difficult situation and tells her how to avoid such situations in the future. The woman then tells others of this ritual, which worked for her. Folk bratas tend to be revelatory in nature—direct revelations by deities to human women.

This is a significant difference between brahmanical bratas of mainstream Hinduism and the nonshastric or nonbrahmanical bratas of folk Hinduism. In the brahmanical bratas, the brata techniques are usually not original—they have already been learned and performed and are simply being retold and passed down to a new audience. For the nonshastric or folk brata stories, the bratas are usually new revelations, coming directly from the deity involved, to help a person in trouble or to punish a wicked person.

In brahmanical Hinduism, this is the difference between shruti (*śruti*) and smriti *(smṛti)*. Shruti is a direct revelation, seen and heard by the person who describes it. Smriti, on the other hand, is indirect, a commentary on or retelling of some more distant event, which is "remembered" by the person who passes it on. For the folk tradition, bratas tend to be shruti, direct revelations, while for brahmanical Hinduism, they are smriti, only secondary sources. This may be in order to emphasize that, for classical Hinduism, there are other texts that are more important revelations: the Vedas, the Upanishads, and often the Epics. However, the folk tradition does not depend on other texts, and brata revelations are primary sources, direct descriptions of revelations by a deity, especially revelations of ritual by which to gain the deity's blessings.

The art historian Pupul Jayakar speaks of bratas (vratas) as a sort of cultural resistance to brahmanical domination, named after the *vrātya* ritualists and magicians of the *Atharva Veda* (these were yogis who fell into trances, later described as wandering sorcerors, who wore black robes and amulets). She describes bratas as mobile rituals independent of temples and specialists, which continued to be practiced during large movements of people retreating from towns to forests and mountains during wars and famines and during migrations from village to village. Bratas gave power and an arena for creativity to women and other disenfranchised groups:

> For the woman, as the main participant and actor of the ritual, the *vrata*s were the umbilical cord which connected her to the furthermost limits of human memories, when woman as priestess and seer guarded the mysteries, the ways of the numinous female. It was around these *vratas,* thousands of variations of which existed in the cities, settled villages and forests, that the rural arts found significant expression. Free of the *brahmanic* canon which demanded discipline and conformity in art and ritual, the *vrata* tradition freed the participant from the inflexible hold of the great tradition. Unlike the *brahmanic* worship of *mantra* and sacrifice, which was available only to the *Brahmin,* the *vrata pūjā* and observances were open to the woman,

to the non-*Brahmin,* to the Śūdra and the tribesman. . . . Many urgencies mingled in the *vrata* rites, providing the channels through which contact with nature and life was maintained and renewed through the worship of the earth, sun, and water and the invoking of the energy of growing things, of trees, plants and animals.[18]

Bratas gave both artistic and religious power to women, who could neither perform ritual temple worship nor join a craft guild:

> The creation of form, the magical act that transformed inert clay into image, was the function of the woman and the craftsman. The woman operated in a magico-religious domain of *maṇḍala* and *vrata* ritual. She painted walls with diagrams, plastered walls with mica and with the auspicious marks of her palm; she molded image and icon. . . . [both she and the craftsman acted as] the link between the monumental forms of the great tradition, the rural gods, and the tribal deities of the forests and the mountains.[19]

Sometimes bratas were associated with mantras and magical spells, with the alpana drawings on the floors and walls taking the role of a tantric mandala or yantra. Jayakar gives a Jungian interpretation to these images, describing them as archetypal images from the collective unconscious which give individuals access to distilled collective memories. However, according to Jayakar, often the stories that came to be associated with these images, the *bratakathās,* contained later brahmanical modifications. These hid the magical origins of the rituals and served to integrate the woman into more mainstream and structured Hindu religious life:

> The *vrata kathās* that today accompany these diagrams, tales lauding the value of the observance and vows and the perils faced by those who neglect to observe them, are later accretions intended to stabilize the magical diagram and to give new interpretations to the imponderables. The *kathās* have become vehicles through which the *brāhmanic* tradition has sought to strengthen its moral and ethical codes that relate to the duties and obligations of women. They deny a woman initiation but leave to her the peripheral rituals. The magical nature of the original act of invocation and transformation persists, but the legends and myths are heavily overloaded with brāhmanic conditioning.[20]

We shall see some examples of brahmanical modifications in bratas shortly, especially the introduction of male brahmin priests, who require expensive gifts and large meals. These changes will be visible in several of the brata stories that will be examined here.

Another, more sociological way to differentiate between folk and brahmanical bratas is in the person who tells the story. Where is the locus of authority?

In the folk bratas, it is the older women of the village who speak to the young women and tell them the stories. Often, all are of lower castes. In the more brahmanical tradition, we have urban *paṇḍit*s, male scholars, who recite the story to upper-class women and perform *pūjā* with Sanskrit mantras. While in the village, the low-caste women are building ponds, making dolls, and organizing ritual pitchers, in the urban areas, the high-caste women tend to be more passive, and the *paṇḍit* performs most of the ritual action.[21]

A French writer interested in folk bratas was J. Helen Rowlands, who also believed that the *aśāstriya* or *laukika* (folk) bratas came from an earlier era. She studied medieval Bengali women, described in Bengali literature. She suggests that it is not only pre-Puranic but pre-Hindu, and followed the idea that they came from the non-Vedic *anyavrata*s. The brahmanical bratas (*śāstriya* or puranic) were introduced to imitate these popular practices, and later to glorify some of the bhakti deities.[22] A more recent book by the German writer Eva Maria Gupta also follows this idea. She believes that the young women's rites have remained close to their roots, while the men's rites have become shastric and changed.[23]

The local origin of bratas appears to be an idea important in Bengali religion, which long resisted brahmanical Hinduism. The idea that most or all bratas have a Vedic origin (described by writers such as P. V. Kane and R. C. Hazra) is less popular among Bengali practitioners, though there are pandits in urban Calcutta who support it. This may be partly due to a certain antibrahmanical feeling in the area, which may have contributed to the rise and popularity of communism in West Bengal.

As Anne Pearson aptly notes on this debate, it is difficult to know what the ancient *anyavrata*s were doing in their rituals, so it is hard to support the folk view. However, the more classical writers downplay the influence of "folk" traditions on "elite" ones, so their claims may also be exaggerated.[24] The safest assumption may be that their ritual forms influenced each other. However, I would argue that since the bratas include new revelations of deities not present in the classical literature, the folk tradition is alive and well, bringing modern revelations like those once brought by Vedic sages.

Bengali writers have been particularly interested in bratas, and characterized them in different ways. Sometimes they are categorized based on who performs them (young girls, married women, all women, men) and sometimes by their origins (brahmanical religious texts or oral tradition). P. K. Maity divides them into customary ("primitive and non-Aryan in origin") and shastric (originating from the *śāstra*s or sacred texts). He believes that the shastric type of brata, for which we have earlier literature, is really a later development with political overtones:

> The *śāstric* bratas, which are few in number, were created later on by the Brahmins who wanted to benefit out of those, either by participating in the priestly function or by taking an upperhand in society. . . . The origin of a

śāstric brata, out of the greed of the Brahmins who act as priests may be illustrated if we see the method of observance of such a *brata,* for instance, the *Harir-charan-brata.* By observing this *brata* a *bratinī* worships the feet of Lord Hari who is the protector of the Universe. A Brahmin priest officiates in this *śāstric brata* and the *bratinī* who observes this *brata* is to give a pair of gold or silver sandals, however small in size, one set of new clothes and *dakshiṇā* (fee) in cash to the Brahmin priest.[25]

Maity contrasts this with the customary or primitive brata, in which women conduct the rituals. There is no involvement of brahmin priests, and no gifts of gold or fees are required. He cites several other scholars who claim a nonAryan origin to the bratas, and argues that these customary bratas were later absorbed into brahmanical Hinduism.

S. R. Das describes the non-brahmanical nature of folk bratas. He emphasizes the importance of the folk or *aśāstriya* (nonshastric) bratas, the bratas that do not follow the Hindu religious books. He states of them:

> *Aśāstriya-vrata* rites have no sanction in the sacred texts. These rites have been current amongst the people from indeterminable times. They are really folk rites preserving the remains of old traditions that go back to prehistoric ages. *Aśāstriya-vrata* rites are not merely childish and meaningless practices but they are replete with certain basic faiths and beliefs of primitive folk-life, translated into rituals that are observed for material benefits.[26]

Despite their brahmanical imagery, these *aśāstriya-vrata*s originate from an earlier culture:

> They are the religious observances neither of the so-called Aryans nor of the later Brahmanas, but of the non-Aryans whom the Aryans described as Dasas, Dasyus, etc., who performed other religious rites and practices (i.e. *anya-vrata*). In the process of aryanization and brahmanisation the non-Aryans were absorbed within the brahmanical fold and their cult, the *Vrata*-rites were assimilated, remnants of which are still to be found in the lower strata of the brahmanical cults and rituals. Even in the so-called *śāstriya-vrata*s which have been sanctioned by the Brahmans and included in the Puranas and in other sacred texts of the Hindus, we find numerous non-Aryan traits and elements. In some cases attempts have been made to veil them with the injunctions of the Puranas and the Tantras.[27]

The shastric/customary brata distinction has also been described by Chittaranjan Ghosh in his *Bāṅglādeser Brata* as a contrast between *paurāṇik* (based in the puranas) and *laukika* (based on folk tradition) bratas.[28] Sankar Sen Gupta suggests a distinction between bratas as *śāstric* (text based and involving both genders) versus *prachalita* (women's rituals).[29] Some brata distinctions are based on participants: Abanindranath Tagore in his *Bāṅglār Brata* gives three groups of bratas: *śāstric, nārī,* and *kumārī* bratas.[30] The *śāstric* group is performed by both genders. The *nārī* bratas are those primarily performed by married women and focus on the health and happiness of husband and children. The *kumārī* bratas are for unmarried girls and are intended to bring a husband who is wealthy and wise. Tagore was interested in the place of bratas as a aspect of folk artistry in popular Bengali culture.

In twentieth-century West Bengal, many bratas are performed in groups of both older and younger women, and all hope together that they may receive the deity's blessings. It is the *kumārī* bratas that are most frequently practiced, according to modern Bengali informants. They are practiced by young girls as part of training for adulthood, and when associated with ritual worship or *pūjā* have been incorporated into festivals (such as the practice of *kumārī pūjā* as a part of the holiday of Durga Puja).

There are several interpretations of the meaning and origin of bratas. Some writers, such as Ray, Jayakar, and Das, see these rituals as the remnants of older Indian religious systems, which were suppressed by the brahmanical orthodoxy. S. K. Ray theorizes that bratas were not only women's religious activity, but in the past belonged to men as well:

> Originally, brata was not a secluded domestic religion for women alone, as we see it today, but existed as an interior wing of a "single and complete magico-religious observance" that also had a powerful exterior wing for men. Somehow or other, the link between the two sexes has now been lost or cut off.[31]

He suggests that the men's branch may survive in such village rituals as the *gājan* (involving ordeals and worship of the god Shiva) and the *jhāpān* rites (religious dances involving snakes). Thus, according to Ray, an originally united religion became segregated by gender. This earlier religion has largely been destroyed—primarily due to invasion of India by alien cultures. He also blames brahmanical Hindu religion for shattering the brata religion. However, the bratas have retained their importance for women:

> The fundamental religion in which the Bengalis are "born and brought up" is called brata. It is a domestic form of religion and apparently not associated with temple service. Bratas are performed exclusively by womenfolk with a view to fulfilling their aspirations by means of magical rites. It can be performed by a single person or by the "elders in assembly" of five married women.[32]

The worship involved in bratas is similar to some ways to brahmanical Hindu worship (*pūjā*). The married woman (*āye*) is the brata priestess of her household—in Ray's words, "a sacred member of (the) village ecclesiastical body of female bratees."[33] No male Hindu priest is required for such worship.

Ray emphasizes the use of animal imagery in the bratas and argues that in the older form of the religion animal deities were worshiped in the rituals. These were later replaced by human forms for the deities, while the animals became clan symbols or ritual mounts (*vāhanas*) that were ridden by the deities. Animal forms are seen on older pitchers (*ghāts*) used in worship, in paintings, and in statues. For instance, Sasthi is a brata goddess associated with child welfare, who rides a cat. Older pictures show her as a cat-headed woman. Other pictures portray the snake goddess Manasa herself with snake hoods, not just holding snakes.

Ray also suggests some historical explanations for deities associated with animals: for instance, the snake goddess Manasa may have been the human queen of a serpent dynasty (a kingdom that made use of serpent imagery), or a foreign invader who conquered Prince Zaratkaru of the indigenous serpent clan and claimed the role of high priestess (in the Manasamangala stories, she is married to the sage Zaratkaru or Jaratkaru, but he fled from her out of fear of her snake ornaments). Ray also suggests that Sitala the smallpox goddess might have originally been a forgotten queen who introduced vaccination via the bags of disease scales often associated with her (Sitala is said in some of her myths to travel with her associate, the god of fevers, and to scatter disease seeds or scales where people have offended her).[34]

Brata rituals are usually (though not always) accompanied by stories, called *kathā*. These stories are generally folktales that contain a moral lesson. The author Sudhansu Kumar Ray divides them into four parts:

1. displeasure of the deity (for nonfulfillment of a promise)
2. trouble caused by the deity
3. fulfillment of the original vow
4. reward for devotion, protection of the devotee, the "mangala incident" in which the deity forgives and blesses the disciple.[35]

We might note that this description is accurate for many bratas, though some do not begin with the deity's displeasure. Instead, they have a person in some sort of trouble, who is rescued and blessed by a deity.

Some writers emphasize that only a limited amount can be said about bratas, for our knowledge of them is poor. T. M. Chatterji writes of this:

These *Vratas*, although they are being celebrated from far-off ages onwards, come down to us only in fragments. We do not find them in the authoritative scriptures but only see them being performed by young ladies and girls in the villages and towns. They naturally differ in minor details in various provinces of Bengal. But the main theme always remains the same. We see in these *Vratas* a true picture of the woman's heart—her desires, fancies and imaginations—a great worship of life unlike the dead ceremonial worship alleged to be based on the scriptures.[36]

He idealizes the vratas as a way for women to be more emotionally expressive and creative, a perspective of religious romanticism. We may also note that he ignores the brahmanical types of bratas described in traditional Hindu sacred literature.

In her recent book *Memoirs of an Indian Woman,* Shudha Mazumdar wrote about her childhood practice of bratas in twentieth-century Calcutta. She explained the reasons for it very clearly:

> Since much would be required of the girl when she attained womanhood, a system of education began to prepare her for her future life from her earliest days. As nearly all things in India hinge on religion, this training was also centered in religious thoughts and practices. It aimed at imparting an elementary knowledge of the basic ideas that were considered by a Bengali family to be good and true; it was accomplished through the medium of little rituals and prayers and fasts. These rituals had some connection with objects that were familiar to the child such as plant and animal life. By this system of training, the child was taught to be disciplined and dutiful and responsible. She who understakes a lesson of this kind is said to have undertaken a *brata.* The literal meaning of *brata* is "vow." So the child takes a vow to do a certain thing which must be performed.[37]

She recalls some of her early practices, with simple Bengali mantras and without priests:

> The *tulsi brata* teaches the child how to care for the bush of sweet basil that is so dearly cherished in every Hindu home. The cow *brata* makes her familiar with the four-footed friend whose milk not only sustained her in infancy but is still an important item of her daily food. There is another delightful *brata* called *punyipukur,* or the lake of merit, in which the child digs a diminutive lake and, seating herself before it, prays to Mother Earth for the gift of tolerance and for the fortitude to endure all things lightly, as does Mother Earth herself.[38]

One good way to learn about the brata tradition is to look at the *bratakathās,* the stories on which the bratas are based. These are directed toward both gods and goddesses, but those toward goddesses seem to be of primary importance to informants interviewed in West Bengal. Let us look at some stories of the vows and fasts taken to please the goddesses and bring good fortune.

4

Some Bengali Bratas to Goddesses

Following are some folk bratas to goddesses, taken from the collection of brata stories and rituals by Gopalcandra Bhattacarya and Rana Debi. This collection was written in Bengali and called *Meyeder Bratakathā*[1] (or *Brata Stories for Girls*). There are many collections of brata stories available in West Bengal, both in bookstores and at temples and shrines. In more rural areas, older women tell the stories and give the ritual instructions, and the books are not necessary. But, with Westernization, people are forgetting the details and turning to books to maintain a link with tradition. This version of the stories was suggested by a Bengali professor, a woman who had used it when she was a child. I have translated here a variety of types of bratas that involve goddesses: some are closer to folk religion, some to brahmanical Hinduism, some focus on distant goddesses and some on human women, and some focus more on magical chants (long repetitions of rhymed poetry or mantras) than on the deities. Major brata goddesses include Durga (forest goddess and victorious warrior), Chandi (earth and fertility goddess), Lakshmi (goddess of happiness, luck, fertility, and wealth), and Sasthi (goddess of children). While brata rituals are traditionally followed by women of all ages, single, married, or widowed, the bratas here are performed especially by young women. These bratas focus primarily on two areas: nature and morality.

Bratas about Nature

Many bratas emphasize the importance of nature and how people who are compassionate toward plants and animals are rewarded. The brata stories show how young women who are kind to other living things are blessed by deities, especially by goddesses. In some bratas girls create ideal worlds, with tiny lakes, rivers, and plant arrangements, as a way to honor nature.

The Puṇyipukur Brata

In this brata, Tulsi is a plant goddess and acts as a folk deity. She is normally associated with the Vaishnava gods Krishna or Vishnu in brahmanical Hinduism. In the Punyipukur (or Purnipukur) brata, however, she acts on her own, with no association to traditional Vaishnava religion, except for the mantra in the first few

Categorizing of bratas

41

lines of the brata. This mantra may well have been a later addition, as it is not related to the story. The writer P. K. Maity specifically notes that the names of Narayana and Brindaban in this brata appear to be a later addition, probably to make the ritual more acceptable to traditional brahmin priests.[2] We also see the use of the term *satī,* here referring to the brahmanical concept of a perfect wife, rather than a wife who enters her husband's funeral pyre.

The female practitioners or *bratinī*s performing this ritual together create a miniature pond, into which they put offerings or pour water. It has been suggested by some observers that this ritual is intended to bring rain, magically causing the ponds and lakes in the area to be filled with rain as the miniature pond is filled. However, today this brata is generically performed for good luck. Earlier versions of this brata have the performer pray to Mother Earth or to the goddess who inhabits a grove of trees.

The brata should begin on the last day of the month of Chaitra and continue through the last day of Baisakh (roughly, the month of May). It should be performed every year for four consecutive years. Every day, early in the morning, the performer should sit facing east. She should draw a square pond (often called a tank in Indian English) with chalk or with her fingers, and place saplings of arum, banana, and wood apple trees over it. She should chant a mantric stanza to the goddess Tulsi, equating her with Brindaban (probably meaning Brindadevi, the goddess of the forests of Brindaban). As the bratini pours water, she should chant this mantra (which focuses upon heaven and salvation) three times:

> Tulsi, Tulsi, Narayana,
> Tulsi, you are Brindaban.
> I pour water onto your head.
> When my life ends, give me a place within you.

Each day the performer should chant these words three times after bathing and offer water to the tulsi plant. There should also be worship at noon, which adds:

> Sacred pond, I worship you with a flower garland (of wood apple
> blossoms).
> I am sati Kalavati, I am the sister of Bhagyavati, of the seven brothers.[3]

She should put sandalwood paste on the flowers and green grass, and then she may add:

> By worshiping (the tulsi) what happens?
> One without wealth becomes wealthy.
> And acquires the attributes of Savitri.
> A woman enjoys the love of her husband
> And bears a healthy son.

She will never have to suffer the pain of Yama (death).
She will die in the holy water of the Ganges (River),
Leaving her son in her husband's lap.[4]

Besides identifying with Kalavati, the heroine of the story, the performer of the brata here also identifies with the mythical character Savitri, who saved her husband's life by outwitting Yama, the lord of death. Savitri is known for her intelligence and bravery. We see brahmanical ideals in her desire to die before her husband while in the Ganges River, and to have her soul go to the heavenly land of Brindaban at death. Performing this brata and worshiping the tulsi plant brings wealth, intelligence, love, a healthy child, and a painless death.

Here is the story which goes along with this ritual:

THE STORY OF THE LAKE OF MERIT

In a remote village there lived a pious brahmin couple. They had only one daughter, named Kalavati. From her childhood days, their daughter used to worship the tulsi tree with great devotion whenever she could find one. She would clean the area around the tree and water it carefully. When the girl reached the age of twelve years, she had a dream one night in which she saw an old brahmin man standing behind her. He said to the girl, "I am deeply impressed by your devotion towards the tulsi plant. From tomorrow, the last day of the month of Chaitra, until the last day of the month of Baisakh, pour a small pitcher of water each day over the tulsi plant and chant mantras, and all your wishes will be fulfilled." Then he vanished. The next day, early in the morning, Kalavati told her vision to her father and mother. Hearing this, her parents told her to follow the instructions of the sage in her dreams.

Beginning the next day, from the last day of Chaitra and the following month, Kalavati dug out a small square pond, and planted in it a sapling of the tulsi plant. She bowed to it (performed *praṇāma*) three times with much devotion. She did this for four years, and on the last day of the month, suddenly an image of a goddess appeared before her. Seeing her Kalavati was very surprised and hesitantly asked who she was.

Taking Kalavati in her own lap, the goddess answered laughingly: "Four years ago I visited you in the form of the old brahmin man in your vision. I told you then to pour water onto the tulsi plant from the last day of Chaitra to the last day of Baisakh. Now four years have passed, your *puṇyipukur brata* has been followed, and you have gained great benefit. I am that tulsi plant. Ask me for a gift."

After bowing to the goddess, Kalavati said, "Mother, let my parents live throughout their lives peacefully." The goddess agreed and said, "Child, that will happen. I shall bless you so that you possess the qualities of Savitri and you will enjoy overflowing happiness and wealth, a husband and children throughout your life." Saying this she vanished.

By the blessings of the goddess, Kalavati got married to Ajit, the only son of a well-known landowner (*zamindar*), in a lavish ceremony. Kalavati's husband and father-in-law gained much wealth and honor, and Kalavati's own parents later had many sons. They never saw the face of poverty since that time. Other women came to know of this brata, and in performing it improved their luck.[5]

This ritual was revealed by the goddess Tulsi, apparently for the first time, when she appeared in the form of a sage (again, this may be a brahmanical addition—the goddess appears as a brahmin man instead of herself). The ritual was a test by the goddess, to see Kalavati's obedience and nurturing ability. By passing the test, Kalavati shows her virtue and gains the goddess' appreciation. Because of the girl's faith and willingness to obey her vision, and her concern for the plant, she is rewarded with even more blessings than she requested. Other women found out about the ritual and copied it themselves, and this is how it spread.

The brata ritual was Tulsi's spontaneous gift for the girl's kindness to her plant form, but other people could follow the ritual. In some districts, there are varying rituals: a deep pool is dug, and other sorts of offerings are placed in the corners of the pool: betel nuts, cowry shells, a type of grass called durba grass, leaves daubed with vermilion and sandalwood paste. In the pool are planted a tulsi plant and branches of the bilva tree. At the end of the brata, an offering is made to frogs, and in other areas, to one or four brahmins.[6]

The Aśvatthapātār Brata

In this brata story, an insulted tree wreaks revenge on a proud girl who was too vain to sit beneath it. The goddess Durga shows the lost girl how to get home and reveals the brata, telling her to propitiate the tree in order to have good fortune. It is observed from the last day of the month of Chaitra until the last day of Baisakh (again, roughly the month of May) by both girls and married women. It is normally performed in a group, for four years in succession.

Women performing the brata ritual (called the *aśvatthapātār brata,* or vow of the leaf of the asvattha or pipal tree), must pick three leaves of each of the following types: budding, green, ripe, dry, and brittle or fallen. The woman should hold these while she immerses herself in water (in a lake, pond, or in the Ganges river). She chants hymns to various deities, asking for blessings on the family: she asks for the wife to sit on a throne of jewels, while the husband rides an elephant. Putting the very young leaf over her head gives her a beautiful young son. Putting the ripe leaf over her head gives her the luck to wear vermilion (and have a husband with a long life), putting the green leaf over her head gives her beauty, putting the dry leaf over her head gives wealth and peace, and the brittle leaf over her head gives great wealth (baskets of gems and pearls). The leaves should then be allowed to float away, and the woman should water the roots of an asvattha tree on her way home, and pray before it.

We see additional influence from brahmanical Hinduism at the end of the ritual. At that time, the woman should offer to a brahmin five asvattha leaves made of gold, one fruit made of silver, and five pitchers made of brass. She should also feed and serve five brahmins and offer them money. In this way, the ritual becomes assimiliated.

The Story of the Asvattha Leaf

In the palace of King Dharmaraj, Kalachand Thakur was the court wise man, or *paṇḍit*. He was wealthy due to his position, and his wife was also very intelligent. Kalachand passed his days happily and had a young daughter. He invited many people to his daughter's *annaprāsana* (the ritual of first serving rice to a child) and held a feast of great splendor. The horoscope reader suggested that he name the child Lajjabati.

As Lajjabati grew older, it grew time to arrange her marriage, and Kalachand Thakur made arrangements with the king to marry her to the prince of the country. Lajjabati became very proud of her future status.

One afternoon she was roaming in her garden with her friends, who called her to sit beneath the Asvattha tree. She refused, saying that it was impossible for her to sit beneath the tree, because crows and ravens stay in it. The Asvattha tree was very hurt by her words, and it silently sighed.

Pride is difficult to tolerate [and causes disaster]. In Dharmaraj's kingdom a famine began, and robbery and dishonesty became widespread. Nobody could prevent it. Every night there were doors and windows smashed and goods taken away, and because of this many people fled the kingdom.

Late one night, thieves robbed the house of Kalachand the wise man. Everything they found, they took away with them. They saw the gold ornaments on Lajjabati, and demanded them from her. Seeing no other way, she unwillingly gave them her ornaments. She began crying, and followed the footsteps of the thieves. She went a long way, and found herself totally lost. She saw an Asvattha tree standing in her path, and prayed to it: "O Asvattha tree, give me shelter inside your trunk." The Asvattha tree [opened up and] gave shelter to Lajjabati.

Lajjabati stayed there, collecting fruits and roots during the day to eat, and then at night sleeping in the tree. One day the goddess Durga saw Lajjabati coming out from the tree, and she approached Lajjabati disguised as an old woman. She asked about her life, and Lajjabati broke into tears as she told what had happened. Durga felt compassionate towards her and said, "Child, don't fear, I'll tell you the way back to your house. You go home, and do as I tell you. Your pride made you look down upon the As-vattha tree, and that is the reason for your unhappiness. You must perform a brata for four years to the Asvattha tree, from the last day of Chaitra to the last day of Baisakh. I will show you how to do this." After Durga showed her the ritual, she disappeared.

Lajjabati found her way home, and returned to her parents. They were very happy to see her again. She followed Durga's advice, and per-formed the brata with asvattha leaves for four years. Gradually her family grew prosperous again, and again arranged to have her married to the prince, whose name was Gunadhara.

Soon, Lajjabati's parents had a son [thus, they were also blessed], and Lajjabati herself had many sons and daughters. Until her old age, she could wear vermilion in her grey hair [showing that her husband was alive], and she lived happily with her family.[7]

Here, the tree is insulted, and this was the reason for the girl's bad luck in life. Though the tree was hurt, it was still forgiving, and allowed the girl to hide safely inside its trunk. The goddess Durga comes, but only to reveal the power of the tree and tell the girl how to please the tree by means of prayer and ritual. By doing the brata to the tree, the girl gained happiness, a good marriage, a brother, and a healthy family. She needed to recognize the power of nature.

The goddess Durga is often associated with plants. During her major Ben-gali holiday, the yearly festival of Durga Puja, Durga is worshiped in a variety of forms. One of these is her Vana Durga, or Durga of the Forest form, made of the *navapatrikā,* or nine plants tied together and shaped into a human female form. While Durga is sometimes herself a tree goddess, here she is merely a helpful by-stander, coming to reveal the brata and disappear. It is the tree itself which dis-tributes good fortune to the girl, and the tree which deserves her reverence.

This is a morality tale, as well as a veiled threat to people who abuse nature. Nature must be respected, or it will take its revenge.

The Jāmāiṣaṣṭhi Brata

The goddess Sasthi, or Jamaisasthi, is the special protectress of children. The Ja-maisasthi brata or Aranyasasthi brata dedicated to her should be performed in the month of Jyestha (roughly, June), on Monday, Tuesday, Friday, or Saturday. It is generally performed by married women during pregnancy—it should not be per-formed by unmarried girls or women who have reached menopause. The brata instructions warn that the ritual must be performed in full—if any woman stops performing the brata in the middle, she will take on the appearance of a female demon. The woman should paint a design on the ground with rice paste (*ālpanā*) and a branch of a banyan tree with a few leaves should be placed next to it with mud, and in front of it should be a small pitcher of water. Over this, she should place banana leaves of the Kathali type of banana, with yogurt on them.

The bratini should make out of dough an image of the goddess Sasthi wearing bracelets, and she should mark it with vermilion paste. An image of a black cat, Sasthi's mount, should also be made of the dough. In a new dish various types of uncut fruits should be offered to the goddess, and a cloth dipped in turmeric water should be tied with six bamboo leaves. Turmeric paste should also be placed on some loose threads, and these and the cloth should be placed near the pitcher. In a second dish should be six leaves of *pān,* six betel nuts, six bananas, six balls of *khir* (milk pudding), and six candies. In a third dish should be coconut balls, lentils, mangoes, sweets, and grains for an offering. Every pregnant woman should do this, and after the offering she should meditate on the goddess Sasthi using a set of mantras. This is a brata story doubtless appreciated by cat owners everywhere.

THE STORY OF THE GREEDY GIRL

A family lived along the shores of a pair of ponds. They had seven sons with seven wives, and the wife of the youngest son was a glutton. Whenever she had a chance, she would steal milk, fish and cream. When the mother asked the wives about this, the youngest wife would say that their black cat had taken the food. Everybody would then beat the poor cat, but the food continued to disappear. Their days passed in this way.

Now the black cat was the mount (*vāhana*) or special animal of the goddess Sasthi. The youngest wife would always blame that cat, and the cat was unable to stand the beatings, so the cat went to Sasthi and complained. The cat would go and report to Sasthi whenever it was beaten. Sasthi promised to take revenge on the youngest wife.

After some months, the youngest wife got pregnant and she bore a beautiful son. The neighbors gave their blessings and went home. When she awoke the next morning, she was unable to find her son. People searched through the whole house, but the child could not be found.

Again the youngest wife got pregnant and had a son. That time also the child was stolen. Each year she bore a son, and each year the child disappeared. Seeing this, the neighbors discussed it with the mother-in-law. "It is very mysterious how the children keep vanishing—she is not ill. Perhaps she is a witch and eats her own children in the night, and then pours out false tears in the morning to delude people."

The young wife overheard this, and decided that when she gave birth to her next child, she would stay awake all night. She soon gave birth to a daughter, and with a heavy heart remained awake through the night, keeping the baby beside her. She stayed awake three nights, but on the fourth night she became sleepy, and felt the child being pulled out of her arms. She opened her eyes, and saw the black cat carrying the child and leaving the room. The young wife quickly got up from the bed and threw her bracelet at the cat. It cut the cat's head, which began to bleed. But the cat kept the child and ran away. The wife followed the cat.

The cat entered a thicket and the young wife could not see ahead, but she followed the marks of blood until she reached a big banyan tree. There she saw the goddess Sasthi squatting. Around her, like a golden crescent, many small children were playing, and the black cat dropped the girl child on Sasthi's lap. The cat said, "O Ma, look what this woman has done to me, she has thrown her bracelet at me and cut my head." The goddess Sasthi then rubbed a lotus leaf gently over the cut area, and the bleeding stopped. The young wife had heard and seen all this from a distance. She came and fell at the feet of Sasthi, crying "See Mother, that cat has taken away six of my sons and this daughter. Please tell your cat to return my children."

Sasthi replied, "Dear child, you do not realize that this cat is my special pet, my *vāhana*. You have stolen milk, fish and cream, and blamed it on this poor cat. Now child, what do you have to say to this?" The young wife asked her forgiveness. Sasthi then said, "First ask for forgiveness from the cat. You must accept your fault in order to get your children back, otherwise you will not get them." The young wife begged forgiveness from the cat, patted it, and admitted her fault. The cat was then benevolent towards her. Sasthi then returned the children to her, and said, "Don't ever beat my cat again, or strike it with a broom or any other object. Don't steal food and blame it on the cat. In every month of Jyestha, at this time, take a branch of a banyan tree, and make a model of the black cat out of dough. Then offer it dishes with every available fruit. During every pregnancy, offer six white pan leaves, six whole betel nuts, six kathali bananas, and six regular bananas. Then perform ritual worship to me. Bathe the banyan branch in a mixture of oil, turmeric paste, and green coconut water. Tie a yellow cloth to six bamboo leaves and keep it in front of a pitcher. And with six loose threads dipped in turmeric, you should make a border around the pitcher. After doing the worship, unfasten the threads and tie them on the arms of the children. Put a dot of oil and turmeric paste mixed with yogurt on their foreheads."

The young wife vowed to both the goddess Sasthi and the cat to do this, and returned to her family with the children. She told the family about the incident and they were very surprised. They were glad to see the children and played with them fondly.

Now, the wives of the other brothers had not yet had any children. Soon after the young wife began her worship of the goddess Sasthi, all the other wives became pregnant and gave birth to sons. Then in the next year they all made arrangements for collective worship of the goddess Sasthi and their wealth began to increase.

Over time, the sons of the youngest wife grew up, and they were married off consecutively. They all brought lively girls [to the household] as their wives. The daughters were married off into rich families. The sons-in-law also participated in the worship of Sasthi, and offered the goddess a big bowl full of mangoes and jackfruit. The blessings of Sasthi gave the family wealth and happiness, and it was full of healthy children. Soon her worship spread, and people far and wide began to worship Sasthi and gain the goddess' blessings.[8]

This story may well derive from earlier folk worship of animals—in this case, cats. It is the cat who is falsely blamed, the cat who wreaks vengeance, and the cat who must be propitiated and worshiped (in the form of a cat made of dough). While the cat is portrayed as Sasthi's servant, in the current version of the brata story it still acts as informer and judge. In the brata, the goddess is to be worshiped in the form of the cat, and she brings fertility to a barren family. Kindness to animals brings reward, while cruelty to one form of life brings the loss of another.

The goal of this brata is to bring good fortune to mothers, as well as gaining the blessings of the goddess. It gives examples of both good and bad behavior. As in the previous story, it is the harmed creature that must forgive the offender. Here the men participate in Sasthi's worship, which is not common in West Bengal today.

The Lakṣmī Brata

Bratas include a variety of goddesses. In rural areas the goddess Lakshmi is very important, for she is an agricultural goddess who gives fertility and wealth to those she blesses. Sudhir Ranjan Das emphasizes the importance of bratas to Lakshmi, normally led by the oldest female member of the group or family, and calls her thrice-yearly bratas "the national festival of the women of Bengal."[9] Especially at her autumn worship, women spend the day making alpana designs and gathering offerings of rice in various pots and baskets, as well as boar's teeth, coconuts, and images of Lakshmi as a plantain plant in a sari.[10]

Usually Lakshmi visits houses voluntarily, but in this *brata* story she is trapped. Her captor is a field spirit from the folk tradition, a *kṣetrapala,* whose traditional work is to guard fields from danger. In this story he is portrayed as a brahmin named Kshetraswami (thus he is called "lord" rather than "guardian"). Though both Lakshmi and her husband Narayana are worshiped in this brata, Narayana has no real power in this story. This brata occurs in the month of Chaitra (from the end of March to the end of April), and the brata collection tells the story but does not list the rituals associated with the brata.

THE STORY OF LAKSHMI'S BONDAGE

Once long ago, Lakshmi and Narayana came down to earth in human form. While roaming the earth, they came across a field of sesame plants. Lakshmi asked Narayana to wait for a minute, and let her pluck some sesame flowers. Narayana warned her against it, saying that if anyone plucked these flowers, he or she would have to cook for twelve years for Kshetraswami, the lord of the field. Lakshmi ignored him and went quickly to the field, plucking flowers and putting them in her hair and around her neck. As she was about to return from the field, Kshetraswami appeared and said, "You must stay here, you cannot return now."

Narayana went to find out why Lakshmi was late and found her wearing the sesame flowers and standing before a brahmin. Narayana asked him why he was detaining her and the brahmin replied, "It is due to my vow—anybody who picks sesame flowers from my field must cook for my family for twelve years." Narayana said, "Lakshmi, you must go (with him). You have received a just reward for your actions." He said to the brahmin, "Since she has taken flowers from your field, she will be a cook in your family for twelve years. Don't serve her with leftovers [an insulting act] or make her wear dirty clothes." Narayana then went away in the chariot and Lakshmi went with the brahmin to his house.

The mistress of the household (*ginni*), on seeing Lakshmi, said to the brahmin, "Where are you bringing this woman from, when we are here half starving?" All of their seven sons and their wives were present. The brahmin said, "Well, dear, if we can get any food, then we can feed her. All of you should give her your love and affection."

The next morning, finding the daughters-in-law sitting idly, Lakshmi exclaimed, "All of you should go and have a bath." The mistress of the house then said, "The men of the house have gone out to beg, let us wait for them to come back." Lakshmi said, "Mother, there is already everything necessary in this house, you should go and see for yourself." On hearing this, everybody went inside the house and found all of the shelves and containers full of food. On seeing this, they wondered if this woman might be a goddess. From that day onward they showed great respect toward Lakshmi.

However, the second wife envied Lakshmi. She was angry when she saw what happened and served Lakshmi with leftovers, which Lakshmi buried near a pomegranate tree. Twelve years passed in this way.

One day, the mistress of the house suggested that Lakshmi should go and bathe in the Ganges River. Lakshmi replied, "You go, I do not feel well. But do me a favor. Give these five cowry shells to Mother Ganga as an offering." The mistress went away with the family, and bathed and performed ritual worship [to the goddess Ganga, goddess of the river]. When she offered Lakshmi's gift, Mother Ganga rose [from the water] and accepted the cowries with her four hands. Seeing this, they realized that their cook was a goddess, and they came running back.

In the meantime, twelve years had passed, and Narayana came with the chariot. As Lakshmi stepped in, the mistress of the house [who had returned] took hold of Lakshmi's feet with tears in her eyes. Lakshmi said, "Stop this, and don't cry. In the months of Bhadra, Kartik, Paush, and Chaitra, worship me, and you will never face poverty. I am Mother Lakshmi, and wealth is lying hidden under the pomegranate tree. You should all share it. For the eldest wife is a silver box, and for the second wife is a box with a necklace inside." Lakshmi then left with Narayana for the heaven worlds.

They went to the pomegranate tree and found a large amount of gold. They realized that the leftovers Lakshmi had buried there had turned into gold. But when the second wife opened her box to get at the necklace, a poisonous snake came out and bit her. This was her reward for her sins. Everybody said, "This is because the second wife got along so badly with Lakshmi."[11] When the eldest wife opened her silver box, golden coins fell from it, as if Lakshmi were giving her gold with open arms. From this incident onward the household began to worship Lakshmi with much devotion. They have never again suffered from poverty. After this, worship of Lakshmi spread far and wide.[12]

We may note that wealth is a sign of a goddess' presence—when the house is suddenly full of food, the family wonders if there is a goddess present there. When another goddess takes Lakshmi's offering, then her presence is proved.

This is a story of punishment and reward—which occurs at both the levels of the gods and the mortals. In this story, a goddess disobeys a rule about nature and must act as a servant, a household cook. Though the god Narayana is present (a form of the pan-Indian god Vishnu), both he and the goddess must obey the rules of the folk deity. The folk deity appears in brahmin guise—perhaps he needed some more acceptable form for his audience, or we have yet another instance of brahmanical influence. However, that influence is limited. The folk god is more powerful than the brahmanical god, partly because both respect the vow that the folk god has taken.

Another brata story is also associated with the Lakṣmī brata. This brata is performed in the month of Bhadra (August–September), and shows the virtue of compassion to animals, especially to Lakshmi's favorite bird, the owl. The goddess Lakshmi may appear to people in a variety of forms. This brata pleases several of these forms of the goddess Lakshmi (Jashalakshmi, Bhagyalakshmi, and Kulalakshmi), and they will stay in the house of the worshiper and bless it. Like the Sasthi story, it emphasizes kindness to animals. It shows a theme that we see in several bratas, a "cargo-cult" approach to wealth. Money is not earned by work, instead it comes miraculously by pleasing the gods. Here palaces, elephants, and jewels come and go spontaneously, unrelated to work or barter.

THE STORY OF THE OWLETS

There once lived a brahmin woman who had a son. She was a widow and very poor. She earned a living by cutting wood (from the forest). There was a banyan tree in front of her hut, and her son used to play day and night under that tree.

One day a vendor selling *khir* (milk pudding) passed by. Seeing him, the little boy wanted to taste some khir. He called to his mother and said, "Mother, give me a coin, I want to buy some khir." The widow answered sadly, "Child, where will I get money? We are very poor." Hearing this, her son started to cry.

The vendor felt sorry for the boy and gave him a little bit of khir and went away. Then who would see the boy's happiness! He sat beneath the banyan tree. In that tree lived a male and female owl with their little ones. On seeing the khir, the owlets began to hoot loudly. Hearing that, the boy climbed the tree and fed the owlets with his khir. He wiped their beaks and put them back into the nest. The boy ate the remaining khir. When the adult owls returned in the evening, they saw the owlets sleeping peacefully. The mother owl asked, "Why don't you shout today? Are you ill?" The owlets said, "No mother, the son of that poor widow has fed us with khir. They are very poor and it is hard for them to get food. Improve their luck." Hearing this, the female owl laughingly said, "All right, children, I will help them. I will tell Lakshmi about this."

The owls went out each morning and returned just before dusk. From that day onward the boy shared half of whatever he could get with the young owls. The owlets told their parents every day about what they ate. Hearing this, the heart of the female owl went out toward the little boy, and she wondered at his behavior. She told her children, "I am going to tell Ma Lakshmi tomorrow."

In the bright half of the month of Bhadra, on Thursday, the brahmin widow made preparations for the ritual worship of Lakshmi. She served the *prasād* (sanctified food) to her only son. The son took it and fed the little owls, and took the leftovers himself. When the adult owls came to the nest, the owlets said, "From this day onward, we will not take any food from you and we will not speak with you. Those living below are very poor, yet the boy feeds us daily from his small share of food. Still you do nothing to help them."

The parent owls said, "You need not fear, their luck has changed. They have worshiped Lakshmi and Narayana with much devotion."

The next morning, when the boy came to the tree, the female owl told the boy, "Your poverty will soon cease. Today I shall take you somewhere, will you go?" The boy agreed, and the female owl then showed the boy a broken branch. She said, "Close your eyes and sit over there, and we owls will carry the branch together and fly. You hold on, and don't be afraid. In the place where we will let you down, if anybody should offer you wealth, don't take it. Instead, ask for the basket of sesame. Then follow wherever the person leads you. You will see stacks of treasure and in the midst of it you will find the basket of sesame. After you receive it, bring it back here to us and sit on this branch again. We will then fly you back home."

The boy followed the words of the owl and closed his eyes. The owls then flew him to the garden of the goddess Lakshmi and asked him to open his eyes. When the boy saw Lakshmi and Narayana there, he wrapped his cloth around his neck and prostrated himself before them. He then stood there with his hands folded. Seeing the boy, Lakshmi felt kind. She affectionately asked, "Who are you, child?" The boy anwered, "Mother, I am very poor. I came here to take the basket of sesame from you." Lakshmi then showed him various types of wealth and invited the boy to take as much as he wanted. But he answered, "No, Mother, I will not take any of these. I ask you to offer me the basket of sesame." Lakshmi then gave the basket of sesame to the boy and said, "Worship this daily and your poverty will disappear and you will gain great wealth." The boy bowed to them again and returned to the branch. The owls then flew him back to his hut.

The boy went inside and called out, "Mother, come quickly!" The widow did not know why he called, but she came quickly. The boy explained the story of the basket of sesame. She then cleaned the house, took out a small pitcher (for the altar), drew alpanas on the wooden seat, and placed the basket of sesame above it. Both of them bowed before it with reverence. Each day they worshiped it with incense sticks and sun-baked rice. The boy told his mother, "Don't tell anybody that we have this basket of sesame."

Soon the grace of Lakshmi showered them, and their luck began to change. They suddenly gained land, wealth, attendants, horses and elephants, palanquins, and other things. Their wealth became so great that it would rival the wealth of a king. The poor widow suddenly gaining this wealth made her neighbors suspicious. One day they saw that she was worshiping a small basket. They went to the king and told him about it. The king thought, "If this old widow becomes so rich, one day she may acquire my kingdom." This disturbed him, and one night the king and his soldiers suddenly attacked the widow's house and stole the basket of sesame. It ended up in the king's cellar, thus making a mockery of Lakshmi's charity. The young boy and his mother lost their wealth and returned to poverty.

The little owls saw what happened, and told their mother, "They are blameless, the king has done this, and as a result they are suffering. Please go again to Lakshmi and bring another basket of sesame." The mother owl answered, "That cannot happen again, my children. If they cannot keep it, there is nothing else I can do." When the little owls heard these words, they began to cry. The mother owl gave in and ultimately took the young boy again to the goddess Lakshmi. He sadly told Lakshmi and Narayana the story. Lakshmi then said, "What can I do? I gave you a gift but you could not keep it. I am giving it to you again—take it." The boy sobbed, and said, "Mother, this time I will keep it safely. No one will know about it." Narayana then said, "Lakshmi, give him a gift once more, and if he cannot keep it, don't give him anything again." Lakshmi then gave him the basket of sesame, and the boy bowed to both of them and left. The owls returned him to his hut.

The boy told everything to his mother. The widow, after bathing, worshiped the basket of sesame secretly. Soon everything was restored and they were able to hold celebrations throughout the year. Seeing this the king became worried again. He was certain that this time his kingdom would be taken over. Seeing no other way, he arranged a marriage between his only daughter and the old widow's son. He gave his daughter a great dowry of wealth, horses, elephants, attendants, and other things.

The widow worshiped Lakshmi every day with great devotion. Though they had wealth, they did not forget to worship for a single day. Soon they could buy much land, and by the age of fourteen years old the boy could become a king. He also made permanent arrangements to feed the two owls and their young ones.

The days passed happily, and the widow grew old. When her time to die came, a chariot of flowers came down from the heavens. Before getting into the chariot, the widow addressed her daughter-in-law: "Dear, in the months of Bhadra, Kartika, Poush, and Chaitra you must worship the goddess Lakshmi. Each day reverently worship the basket of sesame, as I used to do. You will never be unhappy. Another important thing: wake up early in the morning, and never stay late in bed. In the evening offer incense in the prayer room. Don't speak loudly with anybody, and don't make sounds while walking. Throughout your life, remember the names of Lakshmi and Narayana." Then she went into the flower chariot and rode to heaven. Her son made elaborate funeral arrangements for her and invited ten thousand brahmins and the inhabitants of seven villages.

The daughter-in-law followed the rules imparted to her by her mother-in-law, and they had sons and daughters. All of these were married off respectively, as were their own sons and daughters. The kingdom grew richer and richer and was very peaceful. There was no poverty or sorrow in the kingdom. At the death of each generation, the new generation was taught about worshiping Lakshmi and the need to show reverence for her. Thus the world came to know the role of the owls.[13]

Here, as in many European folktales, the boy who is kind to animals is rewarded by them in the end.[14] He respected the owlets to the point of taking their leftovers (a significant act in India). While the parent owls delayed helping the boy, it was their children who forced the issue and blessed the boy and his mother. Again, it is the apparently weak and powerless who generate blessings.

While the deities Lakshmi and Narayana officially hold the power, it is the owls and their children who decide to reward the boy, bring him to heaven, tell him what to request, and again rescue him from poverty after the theft of his magical treasure. One important sign of the boy's virtue as a king: he made permanent arrangements for the owls to be fed.

Nāg Panchamī Brata

Manasa is a folk goddess, the goddess of snakes. Here she becomes a brata goddess, blessing a humble devotee. This brata is performed so that a woman need not fear snakes anymore, and to make her family rich with treasure and servants, during the month of Shraban (July–August). The bratini should fast for a day, bathing at dawn. She should worship a picture or clay statue of a cobra, and a tree branch placed in a pitcher. Saucers of milk are placed by snake holes as offerings, and there is no digging or ploughing of the earth (which might harm snakes). The bratini should also abstain from cutting and grinding food. In some areas of West Bengal, cooking itself is forbidden and the oven is painted with rice powder.

There are similar bratas performed in other areas of India, but they are not dedicated to the goddess Manasa. In this brata, Manasa and Sasthi are allies.

THE BRATA OF MA MANASA, THE SNAKE GODDESS

Once there was a widow who had five sons and five daughters-in-law. The four elder daughters-in-law would sometimes receive gifts and jewelry from their parents' houses, but the youngest daughter-in-law never received any gifts. The other women in the household would insult her because of this, but the youngest girl would tolerate everything—she knew that her father was too poor [to give such gifts].

On the last day of the month, it was raining heavily. The four elder daughters-in-law were talking and playing games. The eldest said to the second eldest, "Oh sister, if someone had cooked some hot rice and lentils, I would certainly eat my fill of it." The second one said, "I would prefer puffed rice and fried vegetables." The third wanted sweets and puffed rice, and the fourth preferred pickled chilis and puffed rice. The youngest sat quietly beside them, but finally said that she would like fermented rice and sour fish. The others laughed at her [this is the sort of food eaten by poor village people].

In the afternoon they all went to the pond to cool off. The youngest was washing a cloth, when she noticed something slither by. She thought it was a fish, so she caught it with her towel. The other sisters-in-law said, "Child, now you can fulfill your desire." The youngest wife put the little thing in a container.

The next day when she removed the cover to see inside the container she realized that it was not a small fish but instead was a small snake. She offered it warm milk and ripe bananas. After eating this, the snake began to move around energetically.

Now, this snake was the son of the goddess Manasa. When it grew bigger, it died and went to heaven. It then explained the plight of the youngest wife to Manasa and Manasa felt sorry for the girl. She took the form of an old woman and went to the house where the widow and her daughters-in-law lived. She found the women of the house insulting the youngest girl because of her father's poverty. On seeing the old woman, the widow asked who she was. Manasa replied that she had come to take the youngest daughter-in-law and the widow said, "You may take her." Then Manasa took her hands and went out to the street. She said, "Child, please close your eyes" and took her to a chariot. Soon they were on their way to heaven.

Manasa then said, "Now you can open your eyes." As soon as the young wife opened her eyes, she could see the small snake, who was moving around. Manasa said, "Child, I am the goddess Mother Manasa. You must worship me every day and feed the snakes with warm milk, but don't go or look toward the south." The young wife answered, "I shall do as you tell me." Saying this, the young wife began to prepare for the worship and served the snakes with warm milk.

One day the young wife forgot the goddess Manasa's directions and looked toward the south. She saw Manasa dancing. She stood looking in astonishment and forgot to warm the milk. When she remembered, she warmed it hurriedly [and made it too hot]. All of the snakes burned their lips. They complained to Mother Manasa and said "We will bite her." Manasa said, "No, don't do that here. First let me take the young wife to her mother-in-law's house and you can go and bite her there." Then Manasa gave her several gold ornaments and left the young wife at her mother-in-law's house. Her relatives rebuked her, but the youngest wife replied, "Let the servant of Sasthi live long. I have worn these ornaments, I shall wear more."

In the meantime, the snakes followed the young wife and overheard her conversation. They told it to the goddess Sasthi, who was impressed with her patience toward her family. Manasa also heard and went to visit the young wife and gave her another set of ornaments. She said, "You must spread my worship around the country. Tell people to place a branch of the Manasa tree and worship it. Those who perform this worship will never suffer from snake bites. After the ritual worship, they may pray to me and ask for a boon."[15]

Again, wealth is a key theme in this story. A wife in the joint household is insulted by the other wives because of her poor background, but her kindness to an animal results in her being blessed. Though she was punished for mild disobedience, her faith in the goddess was rewarded.

This brata is performed on the holiday of Nag Panchami, which celebrates and worships snakes (which are especially associated with ancestors, the underworld, and buried treasure. Nag Panchami is also associated in other areas of India with Krishna's conquest of the great river snake Kaliya. Snakes are a great problem in a rural jungle environment and, in West Bengal, Manasa is worshiped by village people for her ability to cure people of snakebite. Everybody wants to be on her good side, for she is known to be an ill-tempered goddess. Other versions of the brata story emphasize the idea that there must be no cooking on this day, as long ago a woman lit her oven without looking closely and almost killed a snake who was inside.

Some of these brata stories have young people being kind to animals and others obeying them, but nature is always respected. Nature and goddesses are closely related in many of these stories. However, respect for nature is not enough; morality is also an important aspect of the brata tradition.

Bratas about Morality

Some bratas do not focus on the person's relationship to nature, but rather on obedience to a goddess' wishes. Sometimes there is an initial problem (infertility, rejection, disease), other times there is simply a goddess revealing how she may be pleased.

The Mā Goṭhoṣaṣṭhi Brata

In this brata story, the goddess Durga takes on the form of Ma Gothosasthi in order to reveal the proper method for her ritual worship. Her cure for infertility might seem to be a bit extreme to many people. Durga (in disguise) tells the king how to worship her, and it is by his promise to spread the worship that he gets her blessing. In Bengali tradition, goddesses are not too proud to urge people into worshiping them by all sorts of strategems; Manasa in the *Manasa Mangala* stories blackmailed her potential devotees into worshiping her. Here, Durga herself wants worship and goes out to get it. She takes on the name of Sasthi (pronounced Shashthi) of the fields in this story.

This brata is to be performed from the end of the month of Kartik to the end of the month of Agrahayan (November–December), during the full-moon weeks. A brass pot, banyan tree branch, yogurt, oil, turmeric, fruits, and flowers should be offered to the goddess, and the bratini should sculpt dough into the form of grazing fields (*goṭha*) for cows. The woman performing the *brata* should fast, drinking only water, for one day. After she hears the story, she should chant thirteen prayers over a bamboo leaf over the course of twelve months.

THE STORY OF SASTHI OF THE GRAZING FIELDS

Once there was a king who had three queens. However, none of them bore him any children. The king did many sacrifices and other rituals, but still no children were born. Many years passed in this way. The king began to grow old and he brooded day and night over this, praying to the gods.

The king's father and mother died on the same day, and the *śrāddha* (funeral) ceremony had to be performed two days later. The king went hunting and killed many deer and while he was bringing them back with his men a tremendous storm started. Seeing the rain, the king began to ride home quickly on horseback. He saw a hut in the distance, just as he was caught in a heavy downpour. He rode toward it and entered it to take shelter there. Inside he saw an old woman worshiping with a pot, a branch of a banyan tree, and different fruits placed before her. Seeing the king, the woman threw him a grass mat with her left hand, and directed the king to sit on it. The king sat down on it and began to watch the worship with deep concentration. After the ritual was finished, the old woman rose.

The king asked her who she was worshiping. She answered that it was the goddess Mother Gothosasthi. The king asked the goal of the worship and she replied that anyone who performed it would have many sons born at once. Hearing this news, the king rose with much devotion and he went to ask a boon (*mānat*) from Mother Gothosasthi. He vowed that if any of his wives bore him a child he would worship Mother Gothosasthi every year with much pomp and that he would spread her worship around the country.

After some time the rain and thunder stopped and the sun came out. The king wanted to reward the old woman with money but she said that she would not take any from him. She said, "I have no need and I am quite well in this forest." [The brata author adds at this point that the old woman is really the goddess Durga.] When the king returned to his kingdom, he told his wives about the brata. The eldest queen made a mental vow, saying that she wished for a son like the moon.

The funeral ceremony [for the king's parents] was completed, and a year passed by. On the Monday in the month of Kartik that was the day for Mother Gothosasthi's worship, the eldest queen gave much worship to Mother Gothosasthi with the help of a brahmin priest. She repeated her desire [for sons], and took *prasād* [ritual food offered to the goddess, and shared by worshipers].

That year the eldest queen became pregnant. [The other wives are not mentioned, which implies that they did not perform the brata.] When the king received the news, he began to treat the eldest queen very well. He would stay beside her so that she would be happy, and he made arrangements for her to eat any food she wanted. Whatever the eldest queen wanted, the king managed to get for her. When the normal time of pregnancy had passed, the queen had still not given birth. A year passed and the queen's belly was very swollen. The ornaments worn around her waist seemed to get caught in her belly.

Again a year came around, and in the month of Kartik the queen again gave offerings to Mother Gothosasthi and prayed to her. As soon as she completed the prayers, the ornaments around her waist burst. [She gave birth, and] a large sac emerged from her abdomen. The king came running as soon as he heard the news and called the astrologers. They began to draw crosses and charts. They declared, "Great king, inside this sac there are sixty thousand children, all of them yours. The eldest queen is a very auspicious woman."

Hearing this, the king called for the royal midwife. She came and took the sac to the maternity room. When she slit open the mouth of the sac, from inside emerged a large number of boys, as bright as the moon. Seeing this, the king opened the royal treasury and gave gifts to all the poor, blind, lame, and deaf people in his kingdom, as well as to the brahmins and sages. He also gave offerings to a large number of gods and goddesses.

When his sons were six months old, the king held the first rice-feeding ceremony, with great splendor. The sons grew older and the king spread the message of worshiping Mother Gothosasthi throughout the kingdom. And with the beating of drums, he spread the news that those who are still without children should worship this goddess during the bright half of the month of Kartk. One should touch water only after the worship is complete. Gradually the news spread to other kingdoms, and out into the world.[16]

We may note that the king showed patience and respect for the old woman— any object given with the left hand is impure and could easily anger a person of high status. Offering a *mānat* (or *manauti* in Hindi speaking areas) is a common folk practice, especially for men—it basically means a quid pro quo. If the deity will give a specific favor, the worshiper will repay it with worship, offerings, or some other favor. When the king told his wives about the ritual worship described by the old woman, only the eldest queen listened. As a result, only she got pregnant. Thus, we have the combination of male *mānat* and female *brata,* a powerful combination in rural India. It is likely that the 60,000 children simply represent a large number of children (it seems that she got all of the children meant for the other wives as well). Many children is considered to be a blessing in India, the philosophy being "the more, the better." The traditional wedding blessing says, "May you be the mother of a hundred sons." Again, we may note brahmanical influence: Durga did not ask for a brahmin priest to worship her, but one appears at her worship anyway.

The Soubhāgya-chaturthī Brata

This brata is performed at about the same time of year as Durga puja, in the month of Ashvin (September–October), by newly married women and mothers. It commemorates a time when the goddess Durga blessed a devoted but unloved older queen, while the younger queen who was proud and harsh had the land rebel against her. It shows the older ideas of divine kingship, in which the land reflects the ruler's virtues and sins (in this case, with some help from the goddess).

In this brata, Durga is worshiped with a pitcher and with six large leaves of the arum tree. On one leaf, a necklace should be painted in ghee, and on another leaf some dough should be carved into a necklace. Durga is offered incense and prayers, as well as flowers, rice, and vegetables. Later the leaves are thrown into a river or pond. It is to be performed for four years, with the most elaborate worship of Durga in the last year. Again, the goddess Durga reveals her own worship—the ritual is not part of a tradition handed down from the past.

THE STORY OF THE TWO QUEENS

There was a king in ancient times who had two queens: the So-rani and the Do-rani. The Do queen was the elder of the two, and the king did not love her. As she saw no other alternative, she went into the garden and took shelter in an old cattle shed. There she would wear torn saris and sleep on ragged bedding. Yet the younger queen was still not happy, despite her participation in casting out the older queen from the palace. She wanted to exile the older queen from the country and cause her to live in some distant forest. But all of the servants in the palace hated the younger queen, while they loved and admired the older queen.

The younger queen confided her idea of exiling the older queen to a servant, who informed the older queen about it. The older queen was very unhappy to hear about the conspiracy and sobbed throughout the day, losing her interest in food.

It was an auspicious day in the month of Ashvin, and the older queen fasted the whole day and fell asleep at night. Deep in the night she had a vision. An extremely beautiful woman came up to her wearing a red-bordered sari and asked, "Why are you crying? Tomorrow is an important day, and I shall tell you what to do. In the morning get up and bring two arum leaves from the side of the cattleshed. On one of them you should draw a necklace out of pure ghee, and above the leaf put sugar as an offering. On another leaf you should put a necklace molded out of dough, and put some dried uncooked (*ātap*) rice on it as an offering. Then you should call upon Mother Durga, with great devotion. Then cook some food and lay it on the arum leaf with the necklace drawn out of ghee. Then put these into the river. Do all of this with devotion, and your misery will disappear."

The older queen awoke early in the morning and bathed. Then she began to carefully follow the instructions from her dream. She did this for three years, yet her unhappiness remained. Despite her poverty, she never forgot to worship Mother Durga.

Meanwhile, the tyranny of the younger queen increased. She made the servants furious, and they complained to the king. A famine also broke out: in the stables the horses died and in the elephant herds the elephants died. The crops burned and died due to lack of rain. The inhabitants of the country also died due to the lack of food.

All of the ministers and the people praised the older queen. The king heard this and found that everybody missed her. They began to say that the older queen was the Lakshmi (goddess of good fortune) for the kingdom and that it was her departure that had brought in the country's misery. Now there was no way to escape it.

In the fourth year, the older queen did her usual worship of the goddess Durga and with great devotion expressed her wishes to Mother Durga, crying a little. After that she gave offerings and threw the empty leaves into the river. As she was returning, she saw the king approach her from behind a bush. She gasped upon seeing him. He smiled at her and lifted her up, and then he insisted that she come to the palace. The servants were happy to see her, and gradually the famine and problems within the kingdom subsided. There was rainfall again, the land was fertile and peace was restored.

The king called in the younger queen and said: "You were once very anxious to send the older queen into exile. Well, now it is your turn. Pack all of your belongings." The younger queen cried, but the king would not change his mind. The king called a soldier and told him to escort the younger queen into exile.

When the month of Ashvin came again, the older queen offered her worship with much devotion to the goddess Durga. The king heard the story of Durga's greatness with rapt attention. He then spread her worship throughout his kingdom, and from there it went out into the world.

Any woman who performs this brata will live happily ever after. She will never have poverty or misery, and poor women who perform this brata can turn their luck around.[17]

The goddess Durga felt sorry for the ragged and rejected elder queen in this story, and appeared to her in typical Bengali clothing (the red-bordered sari, usually in white cotton). She told the older queen what to do to change her sitation, and the older queen obeyed her. The symbolic offering of jewelry to the goddess (the necklace made of dough), as well as the old queen's faith, brought salvation and her husband's renewed love and respect to the forsaken woman. It took Durga a few years to change the situation, but patience brings reward.

While later understandings of Durga portray her as a heroine and a force of virtue and morality, in her earlier form she is Durga of the Forest, who can bring infertility, famine, and drought if she is displeased. In this case, while it is the king's sin which brings the famine, it is the wrong queen ruling that is bringing nature into disharmony. Durga supports the right queen, who is religious and virtuous, and the return of harmony with nature (making the land fertile, and ending drought and starvation).

The Śītala Ṣaṣṭhi Brata

In the story of Sitala Sasthi, we see the extreme responses of a goddess, in both positive and negative directions. It again appears that a goddess in disguise tells people about her worship so that they may worship her and attain their desires.

This brata saves women from suffering grief and sorrow. In the month of Magh (January–February), at the time of the full moon, on the day of Sasthi, the bratini should worship the goddess. Yogurt, turmeric, and lentils, along with different sorts of fruits and sweets should be offered to Sasthi. Boys (of the household) should have yogurt and turmeric rubbed onto some loose threads, which they should wear.

Sitala means "the cool one," and usually refers to a goddess who brings or cures fever and smallpox. Here we have Sasthi who wants to be worshiped like Sitala, with coolness. On Sasthi's day, the oven should not be used—all cooking should be done the previous day. Lentils and other vegetables should be boiled the day before, and rice should also have been cooked and kept in water. On Sasthi's day, the worshiper should take lentils with the rice and should not take any hot food. The story discusses the reasons for this.

THE STORY OF SASTHI, WHO LOVES COOLNESS

Long ago there lived a brahmin and his wife, the mistress of the household. They had seven sons and seven daughters-in-law, but none of them had any children. The brahmin and his wife were very sad about this, and expressed this to the goddess Sasthi [in prayer].

One day an old woman came there to beg. She saw the mistress of the house talking with her seven daughters-in-law. The old woman asked, "O daughter, how many sons and daughters are there in this house?" The mistress answered, "There are seven daughters-in-law here, yet there are no children." Hearing this, the old woman said, "Dear, don't worry. Just do one thing. On the day of *śuklāṣaṣṭhi,* worship the goddess Sasthi. Then she may shower her blessings upon you." The mistress said, "O mother, how should I perform this worship?"

The old woman said, "Don't take any hot food, or even touch anything hot. Eat fermented rice, lentils, and yogurt. Then you should eat the rice with another vegetable. The night before the worship, you should dig up a stone, and cover it fully with a cloth dipped in turmeric. Then put six dots of vermilion and six dots of white sandalwood paste on it. Keep a *nora* (a type of grinding stone) before the other stone, and offer pairs of bananas, plums, beans, and peas. The next day you should paint the stone with oil, turmeric, and yogurt, and worship it." Saying this, the old woman went away.

So in the month of Magh, on the appointed day, the mistress of the house set up a clay pitcher and dug up a stone. After performing the rituals, she took her daughters-in-law for worship. The in-laws wrapped the corners of their saris around their necks, folded their hands, and said, "Mother Sasthi, have mercy on us. Please look at us, and see that by the turn of this year everyone gets a child in her lap." The goddess blessed them, and all of the daughters-in-law become pregnant at the same time. After ten months and ten days, they all gave birth to attractive sons. The brahmin and his wife were very pleased, and made elaborate arrangements for worship of Sasthi soon after.

They worshiped the goddess Sasthi every year, and got sons every year. Each daughter-in-law gave birth to seven sons. The children grew up, and were married off. Each brought a beautiful bride. The parents grew old, and the burden of the family came to be borne by the sons and daughters-in-law. And each year, the worship of Mother Sasthi was carried out with great care.

In the month of Magh, the day of Sasthi came again. The daughters-in-law and the sons had made the arrangements on the previous day and they completed all cooking during the night. They had poured water on the rice, erected the stone, and had blown a conch shell [to celebrate the worship]. In the morning, however, the mother-in-law said that the day was very cold, that she could not take a both in cold water, and that the daughters-in-law should heat water for a bath and prepare hot food for her to eat. The daughters-in-law looked at each other and began to murmur that today their mother-in-law has become mad, for otherwise she would realize that nobody should light an oven or take hot food on Sitala-Sasthi day. But the mother-in-law insited upon eating hot foods and bathing in hot water. Seeing no other way, the women laid bricks in the courtyard and made an oven and heated water for the bath. The mother-in-law bathed in the hot water and rubbed herself with oil, then ate the hot fish curry, and rice and went to bed, wrapping a quilt around her.

Late at night, the mother-in-law had a nightmare and sprang up from her bed. She tried to wake her husband, sleeping beside her, but he would not wake up. She touched him and found him cold as ice. Then she ran to her sons' room, and yelled from outside, but there was no reply. The dog was lying dead near the front door, as was the cat. In the cattle shed, the cows, goats, and buffaloes were all dead. Seeing this, the woman began to cry out very loudly.

At the sound of her yelling, the neighbors came running. They broke the doors of the rooms and found everyone dead. When the other women heard what had happened, they condemned her for taking the hot food and bath and then went back to their homes.

The mother-in-law began to cry madly and tear out handfuls of her hair. Seeing this, the goddess felt compassionate toward her and came to her again in the form of the old woman. She said sarcastically, "So, you have been eating hot food and bathing in hot water." The mother-in-law fell at her feet and took hold of them, saying, "Ma, please forgive me, without you I am nothing." The goddess Sasthi took pity on her, and said, "There is a grinding stone that was erected by your daughters-in-law, and it was painted with yogurt and turmeric. You should take some of that yogurt and put a dot first on the cat's forehead, then on the dog's, and then on the cow, calf, sons, daughters-in-law, grandsons, and granddaughters. Then you should tie a string dipped in yogurt and turmeric around the hands of your sons, daughters-in-law, grandsons, and granddaughters. In the future, on the day of Sitala-Sasthi, you should not use hot water or (eat) hot foods." Saying this, she vanished.

The mother-in-law did everything that the goddess Sasthi suggested. As soon as she did so, everybody seemed to wake up from sleep. The daughters-in-law said, "Mother, it is late, why didn't you wake us up?" The grandchildren said, "Grandmother, we are feeling very hungry, feed us." The mother-in-law then said, "By the blessings of Mother Sasthi you have regained your lives," and she told them everything that had happened. Hearing all this, her husband became angry and made elaborate preparations for worshiping the goddess Sasthi. The news of her worship spread everywhere and many people performed ritual worship to the goddess Sitala Sasthi with great devotion.[18]

This is clearly a morality tale: obey the goddess and the house is blessed with children; disobey her, and everybody dies. Sasthi is goddess of life and fertility, a gift that she can give or take away if she is not respected. Once people get too lazy for even mild ascetic practicies, they lose faith, and then they lose everything. It may be noted that the cat is Sasthi's special animal (her mount or *vāhana*), and when the humans and animals are raised, it is the cat who gets life first.

In this brata, it is not only faith that is important—ritual makes a real difference. As in Vedic times, ritual procedure needs to be followed exactly.

Lakṣhmīpūjā Brata

There are many folk bratas to Lakshmi, who is another goddess of fertility, as well as luck and wealth. One version of a Lakshmi *brata* has a beginning reminiscent of King Lear: the daughter who answers her father honestly ends up cast out by her father. However, being an auspicious story it lacks the tragic ending. The daughter is blessed by the goddess, who reveals the brata, and the father realizes his false pride. The goal of this brata is to keep the goddess Lakshmi permanently in one's house (thus, bringing luck to the house). While no ritual technique is included for practitioners, except for listening to the story during the month of Kartik, the princess' technique of gaining the goddess' attention was a creative one.

THE STORY OF LAKSHMI'S LIGHTS

In Shantinagar lived a king named Dharmeshwar, and his queen's name was Dharmadasi. The king had five daughters. One day the family and their servants were talking in the palace, and the king asked them, "By whose favor do you live?" Everyone wanted to keep in the king's good graces, so they said "We live due to the mercy of the great king." However, the youngest daughter did not agree to this. She said, "Father, the goddess Lakshmi gives food to all, and human beings have no control over it. People get their food by her grace."

Hearing this, the king became furious. He said, "You have gotten very proud these days. You were not afraid to say such things to me. All right, I will see for myself how your (goddess of) luck provides you with food. Tomorrow morning, I will marry you to the person that I see first. Let us see how much power your Lakshmi possesses." The queen became afraid and forbade everybody in the palace from waking up early. She also told them to go to the marketplace later on.

However, word of the king's promise spread quickly. A poor brahmin man living far away heard about it and thought that though the king might be angry at his daughter, there is no reason that he would give her away without a dowry. He planned accordingly and went to the palace early in the morning, before anyone woke up. He took with him his eighteen-year-old son, whom he told to squat before the king's window, while he hid behind a pillar.

The king woke up and came out. He saw a brahmin boy standing before him and asked what he wanted. The boy said, "Maharaj! You have promised to give your daughter to the first person that you see in the morning. I hope that you will keep your promise." The king then gave his daughter to the boy, along with some dowry. "The king said to her, "Go, my child, you have fed youself at my expense for a long time, now fend for yourself."

The old brahmin left with his son and his daughter-in-law to return to his home in a distant territory, where he lived under a different king. He lived in a hut in a forest, where the mother-in-law accepted the daughter-in-law and took her inside. The princess began to take care of her in-laws and her husband with much devotion. She did not mind living in poverty, and she happily ate any leftovers that remained after the other members of the family had eaten.

One day the princess told her father-in-law and her husband, "Whenever you return from begging, don't return emptyhanded. Even if you don't get anything, at least bring home a handful of grass." They agreed, and one day the brahmin and his son did not get anything from begging. On the way back they found a dead black snake by the side of the road. They brought it home and told the princess the snake was all they could find. The princess said "Fine," and she kept it.

The son of the king of the territory where the brahmin lived was attacked by an unknown disease. The king called healers, charmers, ayurvedic doctors, and quacks from every corner of the country to cure him, but nobody could do it. The child grew worse. A renunciant *sadhu* came and said, "If someone can find me a head of a black snake, then I can help the prince." The news was declared throughout the kingdom with the beating of drums: If anyone could give the head of a black snake, the king would grant him whatever he wishes. The princess heard the sound of the drums, and asked the king's men to come in. She brought down the dead black snake and handed over the head to them. The king's men took it and went away. The sadhu then created medicine from it, and by its use the prince was cured.

The king then called the brahmin [to the palace]. The princess told her father-in-law that if the king wants to give a present, he should not accept it. He should tell the king that if wealth is not given by Lakshmi, it will not come by itself. He should also request that in the month of Kartik, on the new moon night, nobody in the kingdom should light any lights. The brahmin repeated to the king his daughter-in-law's statements, and the king declared that nobody in the kingdom should light a light on that night, or he or she would face punishment.[19]

During the new moon night, the princess fasted and cleaned her hut. She then painted an alpana design on a raised platform, offered flowers, sandalwood, and incense, and lit lamps all around it. She placed mango leaves atop a small pitcher and painted a sun design with vermilion. In this way she prepared for the goddess Lakshmi to come.

Lakshmi flew [through the air] on the back of a female owl [her mount], and when she came down to earth she found that no one had lit any lamps. The owl then began to circle around the area. Suddenly the owl saw a light in a hut and took Lakshmi there. When the princess saw the goddess, she wrapped the end of her sari abound her neck and bowed. Lakshmi asked, "Why is there no light in this territory? Today is the day of my worship, but nobody has lit any lamps. I saw light here, and came down." The princess offered the goddess the raised platform on which to sit and worshiped her with devotion.

The princess chanted praises of Lakshmi and then said: "Mother, we are very poor. We don't have the items required for your worship. With this simple flower and sandalwood, I hope that I may please you."

Lakshmi answered: "Child, I am very pleased by your arrangements. From today onwards, all of your misery will subside. I am leaving my anklet here. In the months of Bhadra, Kartik, Paush, and Chaitra, worship it in remembrance of me. Remember, always remain clean, don't wear dirty clothes, don't abandon courtesy and dharma, don't argue with or scold anybody. Don't tear things with your nails, and don't raise your voice when you speak." Then Lakshmi disappeared. Soon the hut of the brahmin was transformed into a palace with servants, horses, elephants, money, treasure, and much land. Everything became abundant.

The princess called in her father-in-law and said: "Now that we have no more problems and have immense wealth, we should do some good deeds. Please make arrangements to dig a lake." The brahmin did so, and the lake was large and its water was crystal clear. At the celebration of its opening, thousands of brahmins, scholars, and poor people came to a mass feast. Everybody there blessed them.

Meanwhile, the princess' father and family had lost the blessings of Lakshmi. The kingdom, ministers, house, and wealth all disappeared. The king had to beg and stay under a tree. Hearing of the inauguration of the lake, he came with the other poor people and waited with them. The princess was overseeing the arrangements, when she saw her father. She called him to her palace, but he did not recognize her.

She made her father sit on a silver throne and washed his feet, offering him fruits and sweets from a golden dish. He looked at the princess as he ate them and began to sob. Her eyes also became moist. She contained herself and said, "Why do you cry?" The king answered: "Dear, I am crying out of sorrow. I was never like this before. I had a daughter like you and the memory of her is haunting me—that is why I am crying." Could she hold herself back any more? She took hold of her father's feet and cried, saying "Father, I am that girl, I am your daughter. You commanded me to try my luck and I have carried out your command. Now you can see for yourself how Ma Lakshmi provides food to everyone, and human beings are only incidental (*upalakṣya*). Everyone gets his share based on his luck. Mother Lakshmi got angry at you and that is the reason for your present sufferings. From now on, you should worship Mother Lakshmi and you will regain everything."

The king left and returned home. The queen was glad to hear about her daughter and sent men to bring her home [for a visit]. The king began to worship Lakshmi, and by Mother Lakshmi's grace he regained everything. After that he ruled the kingdom happily. Before his death, he invited his daughter and son-in-law to take over ruling the kingdom. In this way, the worship of Lakshmi spread far and wide.[20]

Though the princess was cursed to live in poverty with a mercenary brahmin and his family (and a poor marriage was the major curse a woman could have in India), still her faith in Lakshmi brought her out of poverty and into a renewed relationship with her formerly vain and rejecting father. Though her father accused her of pride, she was humble enough to eat the leftovers of her poor in-laws. She did not have pride, but rather firm faith in the goddess. Here the goddess of luck is also a goddess of family values.

While lights are lit on some holidays to guide ancestors to their living descendents, on the night of Lakshmi's worship (Lakshmi *pūjā*) the lights are for worship and to attract luck to the household. By forbidding the lighting of lamps to the goddess by other people in the kingdom, the princess caused her family and the rest of the kingdom trouble. However, she was rewarded by the goddess and the goddess' anklet brought wealth and land. Lakshmi rewards those who please her but also takes revenge on those who violate her rules, as we see in the next brata story.

Kojāgarī Lakṣmī Brata

The goddess Lakshmi bestows the blessings desired most often by people at all social levels: kings, farmers, merchants, or peasants. In the *Kojāgarī brata,* it is traditional for the worshipers to stay up all night to show their dedication to the goddess. According to some traditions, Lakshmi has a relative (often a sister) named Alakshmi. She is the goddess of poverty and bad luck, and many New Year's rituals involve sweeping Alakshmi out of the house with a broom, thus getting rid of bad luck and inviting in good luck. In Bengali villages, images of Alakshmi are often mistreated in order to please the jealous Lakshmi, for these sisters are rivals. Sometimes Alakshmi may be sculpted of cowdung, dragged through the streets, and humiliated. In other cases, the nose and ears of her image may be chopped off and the image disfigured. Alakshmi is then insulted, leaves the town, and goes off into the forest—sometimes to dwell in an asvattha tree. Once she has gone, good luck will return, for Lakshmi and Alakshmi are mutually exclusive and will not stay in the same house together.

Usually, good behavior is asociated with good luck and bad behavior is associated with misfortune. However, luck and obedience to moral obligation (*dharma*) may sometimes come into conflict. The next brata story explores that conflict.

This brata ritual is performed in honor of the goddess Lakshmi in the month of Ashvin (September–October) on the night of the full moon. People should wear beautiful, clean clothes and listen to the brata story. They should also stay awake and play dice at night, to gain wealth through the year. Such gambling pleases Lakshmi, as it emphasizes the importance of luck, and she blesses the players. Any person who performs this brata will be blessed, for Rajalakshmi (the form of the goddess who blesses kings), Bhagyalakshmi (the goddess of fortune), Kulalakshmi (the goddess who blesses the family), and Jasholakshmi (goddess of good reputation), will stay in the house permanently, and the person who lives there will never be poor.

THE STORY OF FULL-MOON LAKSHMI AND HER LUCK

There once was a king who followed an obligation: he would buy anything remaining unsold in his marketplace, and at the right price. One day a blacksmith brought an iron statue of Alakshmi to sell in the market. But, throughout the day, he sat with it and nobody would buy it. At the end of the day, he took the statue before the palace, calling out for someone who would buy it. The king heard him and bought the statue at its correct price.

That night, the king heard someone crying. He got up from his bed and found the sound coming from the prayer room. The king went into the prayer room and saw a beautiful woman sitting with her head resting on the palm of her hand, crying. The king asked, "Who are you, mother? Why are you crying?" The woman said, "I am Rajalakshmi, and I have stayed for a long time in your house. Now I cannot stay any more, and I am crying." The king asked, "But what wrong have I done?" Rajalakshmi answered: "Why, you have caused me to leave. You have brought Alakshmi into this house. That is why I must go. I am saddened that I must go, for I have been in this house for a long time. As I leave, I will give you a boon—from now on you will be able to understand the language of all animals and plants. But do not tell anyone of this, or you will die." Saying this, Rajalakshmi departed.

The king went back to his bedroom, but he could not go back to sleep. He sat beside the window thinking and saw someone walking out of the palace. He ran outside and asked, "Who are you, mother?" She answered: "I am Bhagyalakshmi. You have brought Alakshmi into this house, so I am leaving." Hearing this the king stood still with his head down. He saw another beautiful woman leaving the palace. The king asked who she was, and she answered: "I am Jasholakshmi. Why did you bring Alakshmi here? That is why I am leaving." Then all three of them left the palace as the night ended.

The next night the king saw a beautiful couple leaving the palace. Seeing them, the king ran outside and stopped them. He asked who they were and why they were out so late at night. The woman said, "I am Kulalakshmi, and I am leaving because of Alakshmi." The man answered, "I am Dharma, and I am also leaving you because of Alakshmi." Hearing this, the king knelt down before Dharma, and asked: "What is my sin? I kept my promise and, following my obligations, I bought Alakshmi, you know that. Dharma is my strength. In order to follow dharma, I lost Rajalakshmi, Bhagyalakshmi, Jasholakshmi, and now Kulalakshmi. I am dedicated to dharma (correct moral action) and I have not violated it. I cannot let you go." The god Dharma [thought about this, and he] found that the king was right, so he stayed. Kulalakshmi went away alone.

Over time, the king's life began to deteriorate. When one is without Lakshmi, how can he or she have peace? The king became weak and the queen was frightened. She began to sit by herself beside the king and she herself served her husband whatever was cooked. Whenever the king sat down to eat, swarms of ants would gather around his dishes. After several days the king lost his appetite. He asked the queen not to put any ghee in his food, so she fed him food without it. Even the ants then found his food unappealing. The leader of the ants said, "See, because of that Alakshmi, the king has become so poor that he cannot even afford ghee!" Hearing this, the king began to laugh. The queen asked why he was laughing, but he wouldn't say. The king said: "My dear, if I tell you, I will die immediately. I cannot speak of it." The queen continued to ask him, so the king said: "Well, if my death brings you happiness, then let's go to the river bank. I will explain there."

They went to the river bank, and the king asked, "Is it really necessary for you to know this, even knowing that I will die if I tell you?" The queen said, "Yes, I must know." The queen didn't actually believe that the king would die—how could someone die just by revealing something?

Suddenly the king saw a female jackal next to a male jackal. The female jackal pointed to a corpse floating in the river. She asked, "Why don't you bring it here, so we can eat it?" The male jackal answered, "I am not a fool like the king, listening to the queen's words." After overhearing this conversation, the king left the queen and ran toward his palace, leaving the queen to roam alone by the river bank.

She stayed there for a long time [feeling rejected by the king], and one evening in the month of Ashvin, during a full moon night, the queen heard the sound of a conch shell [being blown] and a bell. She went toward it and saw men and women worshiping the goddess Lakshmi. The goddess' form was made from banana leaves. When she asked the people, "What god are you worshiping?" they were surprised and said: "You don't know who this goddess is? This is the ritual worship of the goddess Lakshmi, and anyone who performs it causes Lakshmi to come and Alakshmi to leave." The queen participated in their worship, and shaped her own form of Lakshmi using a mold. They offered grated coconut, rice flakes, and other items of worship. After the worship they ate it themselves and also shared some with the queen. The queen stayed awake the whole night listening to the singing and storytelling.

The next morning, the iron statue of Alakshmi disappeared from the prayer room of the palace. Nobody saw where it went. The god Dharma told the king to bring back the queen to the palace, for the days of his curse had ended. The king immediately made arrangements to bring back the queen and later made elaborate arrangements for Lakshmi's worship. Eventually Bhagyalakshmi, Jasholakshmi, Rajalakshmi, and Kulalakshmi returned to the palace.

From that time, worship of Lakshmi spread far and wide. Anyone who worships Lakshmi in this way never suffers from misery or poverty.[21]

In this story, the king's practice of following dharma (as proper moral and ritual action) comes into conflict with the will of Dharma (the god). The king must argue that his previous dharmic obligation (to buy goods) took priority over his later and conflicting dharmic obligation (not to buy the goods, specifically the statue of Alakshmi). The presence of Alakshmi, goddess of bad luck and poverty, chases out the goddesses of royal luck and fortune and curses the king. Though the queen's curiosity endangered the king's life (and we have here a clear example of a negative stereotype about women and their curiosity), nevertheless the queen's brata of staying awake all night and worshiping Lakshmi returned the king's lost fortunes. As the brata story makes clear, even women with many faults can help and save their husbands if they properly perform the brata to the goddess.

The Brata of Maṅgalu Saṅkrānti

Some bratas have a great focus on ritual purity. The brata of Mangala Sankranti should be followed in the month of Jyestha (May–June). It makes the performer immune to impurity. It also shows some of the stranger conditions that can result from the state of impurity. The savioress in this case is a woman renunciant, a *sannyāsinī*, who reveals both the problem and the cure. The brata ritual involves worship of the goddess Mangalachandi, an auspicious form of the folk goddess Chandi. She is worshiped with betel nuts, durba grass, alpana, pitcher, and several ritual objects. Worship of Mangalachandi, a goddess whose powers are great and transcend purity and impurity, wipes away the negative results of impurity. This brata also shows a positive mother-in-law/ daughter-in-law relationship, a relationship that is traditionally one of great stress in India.[22]

This brata story is heavily influenced by brahmanical Hinduism—it involves ritual worship (*pūjā*), the importance of purity and impurity, brahmin protagonists, and renunciation. The brata is described in the story as an existing ritual rather than the revelation of a new ritual. However, the original form of this curious brata appears to be older: we have a woman who touches objects and persons while she is in an impure state, becoming possessed by them and taking on their forms. Such possession and involuntary shape-shifting are not found in brahmanical Hinduism, though we do see these themes in Indian folklore.

THE STORY OF THE DISEASES OF IMPURITY

There lived in this country a very poor brahmin man and life was difficult for him. His family consisted of himself, his wife, and his mother. One day he told his wife: "Without money, we cannot survive as a family. Therefore I think I shall go to the palace and see if I can get money there. You should look after my mother in the meantime, so that she does not feel neglected." Saying this, the brahmin left. His wife took good care of her mother-in-law. But regardless of her care, the mother-in-law began to grow thin like a dry stick. The wife grew frightened and wondered how this could be, for she fed the older woman well, on much milk, ghee, and yogurt.

As three or four months passed, the wife began to wonder what she would say to her husband when he returned. Would he accuse her of trying to starve her mother-in-law to death? How could such a thing be? She found herself unable to sleep at night with worry.

One evening, the wife went to bed after completing her household chores, leaving the window facing the courtyard open. It was a full-moon night and the moonlight shone brightly in her room. She was lying in bed thinking of her mother-in-law when she noticed that her mother-in-law had left her room and gone into the courtyard. The mother-in-law suddenly changed her form, becoming a copper dish that rotated through the courtyard. The wife was shocked to see this. It was about midnight. The mother-in-law returned to her room and again went out into the courtyard, changed her form into a sacred thread, and began to rotate like a top. Then she went back to her room. The wife was starting to feel tired and she wondered, who does one ask about such things?

Then in the third quarter of the night, the mother-in-law came out and turned into a conch shell, again circling the courtyard. By now the wife was getting annoyed and no longer felt sleepy. She sat beside the window wondering what to do. Just before dawn, the mother-in-law came out again, and this time she turned into a cow, who roamed around the courtyard making noise. After a while, she returned to her room.

At daybreak, the wife got up and started doing her daily chores, including sweeping the courtyard. Then she did the dishes and went to bathe. That day her husband returned, bringing with him two servants. They carried rice, lentils, oil, wheat flour, ghee, clothing, and other things. The brahmin also brought back a large amount of money. She took everything into their storeroom. The brahmin bathed and then went to his mother's room. He was shocked at seeing his mother's condition and fell backward.

When he asked his wife what had happened, she replied that she had cared well for his mother and could not figure out why the mother was getting emaciated. She said: "I have been bothered by this for the last two months. Last night I was sleepless and I looked outside my window. I saw in the first quarter (of the night) that Mother, in the form of a copper dish, was circling around the courtyard. In the second quarter she turned herself into a sacred thread, in the third and fourth quarters she turned herself into a conch shell and a cow. Seeing this, I was quite astounded."

The brahmin also felt surprised. Then after a bath, chanting some hymns, and a meal, he went to the *tol* (a center for the knowledgable people of the village) where he spoke frankly to the elders. After listening to the story, they said that they had never heard of any disease like this before. The brahmin returned home and asked his mother if his wife had taken good care of her. She said: "Yes, my child, she took good care of me. She used to cook many types of food for me, and would serve me a big bowl of milk twice a day. Why do you ask?" The brahmin answered: "For no reason in particular—after all, she is someone else's daughter. But it looks like you have not eaten for a long time. Do you have some disease?"

His mother answered, "No, my son, I don't feel anything." But the brahmin did not believe this. He told his wife, "I am going out to find medicines to cure my mother, and I won't come back until I find them." Saying this, the brahmin left.

At midday, he found a female renunciant (*sannyāsinī*) meditating beneath a banyan tree. The sannyasini was deep in trance. The brahmin wrapped his cloth around his neck and sat before her, with his hands folded.

In the evening, her meditation ended. The brahmin bowed to her and addressed her as Mother [thus creating a relationship between them]. He said, "Mother, you know all things. My [own] mother is suffering from a mysterious disease that we do not understand." Then the brahmin told her the whole story. The sannyāsinī then replied, "The reason for this disorder is impurity. If anyone in an impure condition touches copper, a brahmin man, a conch shell, and a cow, this disorder results. To cure this, a person must perform the Mangala Sankranti brata with betel nut, and drink the water after dipping the betel nut (into it)."

The brahmin asked, "Where shall I get the betel nut, Ma?" The sannyāsinī then answered: "In the land of Mangala, the queen performs the Mangala Sankranti brata. If you can see her, you may cure your mother. But the queen must give you her betel nut."

The brahmin bowed to her [and set out on his journey]. Soon he reached the palace of Mangala. He went to the king's court and was welcomed by the king. Seeing that he was tired, the king ordered food for him. The brahmin said: "Great king, I have been without food for the last four days, and I came here by foot from far away. If you satisfy my wishes, I shall eat your food, but otherwise not." The king said, "Oh, you have been fast-ing for four days, and now you say that you won't take any food! This is strange. Tell me what it is that you want. If it is within my power, I will give it to you."

The brahmin told him what had happened, and the advice of the san-nyāsinī. The king answered, "These [nuts] are not my property. They are owned by my queen and I have no control over them. But if she gives her consent, then you will get the betel nut. In the meantime, you should go and bathe and have something to eat." The brahmin replied: "No, not yet. If the queen gives her consent, then I shall eat, otherwise I shall starve to death right here."

The queen, sitting in her great bed, was watching the moon. The king came and sat beside the queen and told her the brahmin's story. She said, "Well, if there are more than 108 betel nuts in my casket, then I can give one." She opened her golden casket and found that there were 109 betel nuts. She handed one over to the king and told him to give it to the brah-min. She said: "In the month of Jyestha, on the last day of the month, a whole betel and eight bunches of grass, dipped in red *alta* (a paint made from lac) are to be wrapped with a red cord. Then alpana should be painted on the floor, and a small pitcher is to be placed at the center. One should then per-form ritual worship to (the goddess) Mangalachandi with the help of a brah-min. After the betel nut is dipped into the water (in the pitcher), the water should then be drunk by the brahmin's mother. She will then be cured. But this must be done in a month with an even number of days. If the number of days in Jyestha turns out to be uneven, then she must do this in a differ-ent month."

The king returned to the court and gave the betel nut to the brahmin, telling him the instructions. The brahmin agreed to eat and then began his return journey. Upon his return, he explained the queen's instructions and gave his wife the betel nut. She then painted the alpana design with a cloth, placed the pitcher, and dedicated the ritual to Mangalachandi in the name of her mother-in-law and herself. After the ritual worship, she dipped the betel nut, and gave her mother-in-law the water. Within four or five days, the mother-in-law was cured. The women in the village found out about this brata, and they began to practice it themselves.

If a woman performs this brata, no matter what she touches in an im-pure state, she will not suffer from any illness as a result.[23]

In this brata story, the wife and mother-in-law appear to get along well, de-spite the husband's suspicions. There is often a clash of loyalties for the man— should he love his mother or his wife more? Here the information about the brata given by the sannyasini, with objects later gathered by the husband and ritual performed by the wife, save the brahmin's mother. The brata has the family working together to save one of its members.

As a note, it is considered bad behavior for a host to have visitors who are hungry and not fed. It violates the ethic of hospitality. The brahmin uses this ethic of hospitality against the king to get what he wants, basically blackmailing the king into giving him the betel nuts.

There are many folktales in the world that involve shape shifting or changing form by supernatural beings, but it is rare to see this afflict someone involuntarily (except, perhaps, with the popularity of stories of werewolves). It may be that the prebrahmanical version of this story involved not impurity but violations of a deity's commands, with this type of shape shifting as a curse.

The Brata of Bipattārinī

Many of the brata stories have heroines as major characters. Sometimes they are human savioresses, and sometimes divine ones. The goddess Bipattarini (or Bipadtarini), whose name means "the goddess who saves from danger," is usually understood to be a form of the goddess Kali or Durga (in West Bengal, these goddesses are often equated). Here, Kali/Durga saves Shiva from the poison he swallowed at the churning of the world ocean—a story line similar to that of the Tara story at Tarapith (a *śaktu pīṭha* or site sacred to the goddess, located in West Bengal). The goddess Durga also protects the god Krishna, thus showing the power of Shaktism over Vaishnavism. Any woman who performs this brata gets the blessings of Bipattarini and averts disaster from herself and her family. The story involves the sage Narada, the universal traveler, busybody and gossip of the gods. He reveals the origin of the title "Savioress from Danger."

This brata should be performed in the month of Ashar (June—July), on any Saturday or Tuesday, between the holidays of Rathyatra and Ultarath. On the day before the brata day, the woman must eat only vegetarian dishes, and on the day of the brata she must fast. She must serve nine types of fruits to the goddess Bipattarini and wear red threads with fourteen knots on her left hand. If men participate, they must wear the red threads on their right hands.

THE STORY OF THE GODDESS WHO SAVES PEOPLE FROM DANGER

One day while the sage Narada was exploring the world, he reached the banks of the river Karotowa. He saw about a dozen women collectively worshiping the goddess Durga, and some were chanting her name 800 times. The women asked Narada: "Why does Ma Durga also have the name Bipattarini Ma (protectress from danger)? Please tell us the story."

Narada answered: "All right, listen, and I will explain why Devi Durga is also called Bipattarini Ma. When the *asuras* [a form of enemy or demon, described in Vedic literature] were skimming the treasures from the sea, they encountered the Kalakut poison, the poison Shiva Mahadeva swallowed while meditating on the goddess Durga. Durga saved Shiva from that danger, and thus she was called Bipattarini.

According to another story, Yashoda [Krishna's adoptive mother] used to tie an amulet around the hand of the young Krishna. It was an amulet of the goddess Durga, to prevent anything evil happening to Krishna. Whenever Krishna faced danger, he could overcome it by chanting the name of Mother Durga. Indeed, it was while chanting Durga, Durga, that Krishna attacked the serpent Kalidaha and was able to defeat it. Since Ma Durga has saved Krishna many times, she has also been called Ma Bipattarini.[24]

This brata shows the influence of brahmanical Hinduism, as its story of the churning of the milk ocean to create nectar and poison is described in both the Vedas and puranas. When the ocean was churned in the beginning of time, an intense poison was created, the Kalakut poison. It would have destroyed the world, so the god Shiva swallowed it. It turned his throat blue (thus his title Nilakantha, the blue-throated one) but he saved the world. According to this version of the story, Shiva was saved from death because he meditated on the goddess Durga. Thus, the god Shiva is saved by the goddess Durga (who is also his wife, according to Bengali myth), and the goddess is shown to be more powerful than the god. The god Krishna, too, was dependent on Durga's strength to save him, especially during his childhood. She saved Krishna, the high god of the Bengali Vaishnavas, and thus the god of a rival sect. The question of "who saves who" is often a very political one.

The goddess Durga has been of aid to Vaishnava deities in other situations. According to Bengali tradition, Durga also allowed Rama to conquer the demon Ravana in the *Ramayana* by her grace, for Rama was not strong enough to conquer him alone. In Krittivasa's *Adbhuta Ramayana,* Sita turns into Kali/Durga to defeat a stronger relative of Ravana, named Mahi Ravana, whom Rama was unable to best in combat.

According to another brata story, Durga saves the queen of Vidarbha from the effects of her own curiosity. The queen told her friend, was the wife of a shoemaker, that she wanted to see [and taste] beef. She asked the shoemaker's wife to bring her some secretly. The shoemaker's wife brought her the beef, but a guard saw her with it and told the king. The king questioned the queen, who said that the woman had only brought her fruit and flowers. She then prayed to the goddess Durga to rescue her, and Durga did so by turning the meat into fruit and flowers. The king examined the food and saw that there was no beef, and he left satisfied. The queen was grateful to Durga for her intervention and decided to observe a brata ritual to Durga in her role as saviouress and remover of disaster. Others observed her and followed suit, and the ritual spread.[25]

We may note that eating beef is not acceptable behavior for brahmanical Hinduism, but this clearly does not bother Durga (who has folk aspects which accept blood sacrifice). Here she is not the Sanskritic goddess of virtue and heroism, but rather a friend. Devotion is more important than brahmanical rules, and this form of Durga is a folk goddess willing to help her erring devotees out of trouble.

All of these stories teach moral lessons, ritual practice, and the virtue of devotion and asceticism to the young women who hear the stories recited or read from the *brata* collection. Some themes that we see in these stories:

1. Gods and goddesses are like human beings, they make mistakes and suffer for them. They are also bound by the rules of *dharma,* and violation of these universal laws brings them punishment.
2. Gods and goddesses can take on human form and communicate their desires to human beings. One need not wait for a traditional *avatar,* or Hindu incarnation of a god. Folk goddesses and gods may be nearby, in disguise as an old woman or a brahmin man.
3. Gods and goddesses need respect and worship. They are unhappy when they are ignored and might be inclined to punish people too proud to worship them. Humans need gods, but gods also need human beings.
4. Nature also needs respect and worship. Sometimes it is personified as a goddess (Mother Earth or Prakriti), and sometimes it is a specific creature or the sum total of natural phenomena, but in any case, treating nature badly brings unhappiness and bad luck.
5. Gods and goddesses often want ritual worship, or *pūjā,* from their devotees. However, this process of mantras and offerings is not the only sort of worship desired. Sometimes deities are arbitrary in their preferences, asking for tree branches, strings soaked in yogurt and turmeric, miniature ponds, and images made of dough. Sometimes these forms of worship are connected to past mythologies and sometimes they are new desires, for deities in the folk tradition are understood to grow and change (for instance, the goddess Durga who during the nine nights of Durga puja wants to take on new deity forms or *rūpas,* and is worshiped in various guises in rural West Bengal). The various desires of the deities are revealed in the brata stories.

Worship of deities in Hindu tradition may be monotheistic or polytheistic. In monotheistic traditions (especially some forms of Vaishnavism), only one god is worshiped and considered to be the only true god. In more polytheistic traditions, the devotee may worship both the family god (or *kuladevatā*) and a personal, chosen god (or *iṣṭadevatā*), as well as others. When a young woman leaves her parents' house to live with her husband's family, her family deity changes (to the deity of her husband's family), but her personal deity remains the same.

6. Fasting, not bathing, or other forms of mild asceticism are valued by the gods and goddesses, for they show devotion. In India, fasting does not always mean total avoidance of all food and drink. One may do partial fasting, such as not eating hot things or cold things or sun-dried rice or drinking milk. While the term "brata" is often translated as "fast," the rules for many of these stories do not specify fasting (though a few informants said that bratas always have fasting, whether the story and ritual says so or not). In general, it seems to be more important for the young women to hear the stories of the gods and goddesses, worship them, and give them offerings.

7. The emphasis on devotion or *bhakti* is marked in many of these stories. Deities want obedience but they also want love, as shown through the various ritual practices (including listening to the stories). Such ritual is understood to maintain and express love, and thus make the gods and goddesses happy and full of blessings.

While goddesses are a major focus of brata rituals in West Bengal, there are also other bratas directed to gods, to human women, and to animals with supernatural powers. There are also bratas not directed toward any particular character. These depend on the bratini's emotions and force of will, and the magical use of objects.

5

Other Bratas:
Women, Nature, Gods, and Magic

Some bratas are not dedicated to supernatural deities but rather to living ones: women who are viewed as particularly fortunate. Two that will be described here are dedicated to auspicious wives, those whose husbands are alive and healthy (according to informants, this brata focuses especially on older wives), and another is dedicated to young virgins, who are auspicious for their potential. A highly valued skill of such "human goddesses" is the ability to save their husbands from the negative results of the husband's bad karma. Such bratas emphasize the importance of women for each other and for their families, as well as the role of community for women.

Female Community

Following are a set of bratas performed to living women on the spring holiday of Akshaya Tritiya, which is commonly celebrated as a day of worship of the goddess Lakshmi, who represents luck. While most bratas have stories (*kathā*), these have only the ritual practices (*niyama*), which describe the worship performed by both young girls and older women. There are several variants of the *akṣaya—ṭritīyā brata,* which focus on the fortune and abilities of women. They involve the worship of a living woman who represents a goddess and who is offered gifts and believed to be able to bestow blessings. They are unusual bratas in that there are no stories, no moral lessons, no gods and goddesses, and little submission to traditional roles.

Brata to Auspicious Older Women

The *āda-holud brata,* or the brata of ginger and turmeric, is performed from the last day of the month of Chaitra to the last day of the month of Baisakh (roughly, the month of May), and should be continued for four years. It is the worship of fortunate women, who are called *āyes.* Such women may be of any age, but are often old. A woman whose husband is alive should be chosen, and she should be offered a handful of unhusked rice, and of coriander, as well as five pieces of ginger and five of fresh turmeric. She should also be offered sweets (*sandesh,* or small cheesecakes) and a small amount of money. The end of the fourth year is a time of celebration, and four auspicious wives should be invited. They should be feasted, given iron bracelets (*loha,* traditionally worn by Bengali wives), vermilion, a vermilion jar, *āltā* paint (a red liquid for decorating the feet), a brush, and if possible a sari and cloth. The original woman served should also be given iron bracelets twisted with gold, and fan, a sari, a comb, and more money. The goal of this brata is to guarantee that the woman who performs it will never be a widow.[1] She will live a fortunate and happy life, like the wives worshiped.

Another brata is called the *ādar singhāsana brata,* or brata of the throne of love or honor. A beautiful woman is found who has been fortunate in love and is happily married. She has no rivals and has never been disappointed. She sits on a wooden seat or "throne" decorated with alpana designs, while flowers and fruits are offered to her. The goal of doing so is for the women offering her the objects to be happy in love, as she has been.[2]

These rituals appreciate mature women, worshiping them as goddesses. Their fortune in life shows that they have a large supply of luck, which may be shared.

The Young Maiden Brata

Other bratas are dedicated to young girls, such as this variation on the worship of young girls, or *kumārī pūjā.*[3] It is called the *akṣaya-kumārī brata* or the brata to the young maiden, and it is to be performed every year for four years on the *akṣaya-tritīyā* day. On this day, the person performing the brata should invite a young girl to sit on a low, wooden stool. The girl's feet should be washed and then painted with red *āltā* liquid. Then she should be wrapped in a sari with a red border and her hair combed. The woman performing the brata should then paint dots of white sandalwood paste and vermilion on her forehead and feed her lavishly. This should be done each of the four years. In the last year, the young girl and three other girls are to be invited for a good meal. They should be given saris with red borders, hair brushes, *āltā* liquid, comb, mirror, and small gifts of money. The girl who was invited for the four consecutive years should receive more money and an extra cloth. The girls should have their feet washed and should put on their new saris. It is said that this brata gives good fortune, and also the blessings of Mahamaya, the great goddess.[4]

Here we have a ritual to young girls, who are often ignored and unappreciated in the family setting for they will be married off and leave the family and a dowry will be required for their marriage. This ritual shows them to be sources of good fortune and capable of bestowing blessings on others. Kumari puja is also performed during the Durga Puja, the nine-night celebration, which is the biggest holiday in West Bengal. It is a great honor for the girls chosen. However, the

Durga Puja version of the ritual usually has a large audience, rather than involving only a few participants, and is a public event.

One brata story associated with *akshaya-tritīyā* shows a wife's ability to save her husband from damnation, due to her own generosity on earth. The auspicious wife is worshiped because she is believed to have great fortune and power, even against the forces of the underworld. Again, in the folk tradition, her power is a result of her own actions and it does not come from any deity (and certainly not from her husband).

This is in many ways an antibrahmanical story, though it uses brahmanical imagery.

THE WIFE WHO SAVED HER HUSBAND FROM HELL

In ancient times there was a brahmin who was an atheist. He was intelligent, but ill-mannered. He had a devoted wife who was named Sushila. One day a hungry sage came to his house, with throat parched from thirst and hunger. He asked the brahmin householder, "Please sir, save my life with a little food and water." The furious brahmin chased him out, telling him to go elsewhere, that he had no food or water, or even a place for him to sit.

As the embarrassed traveler was leaving, the wife called to him with a soft voice. "Lord, please don't be angry and leave. Stay here and I shall bring you some food and water." She asked her husband, "What is the good of wealth and an attractive house if guests are turned away? Service to man is, after all, service to God." She then gave the traveler food and water.

A few days later, the intelligent brahmin died. Yamaduta [the messenger of Yama, Lord of the Underworld] then took him to the underworld, and threw him into hell, where he was punished severely for his bad actions. When the brahmin was in extreme pain, he shouted for water, but Yamaduta answered, "Hey, evil-face, while you were alive you denied water to a traveling guest. Now suffer the fruits of your deed."

Yamaduta then took the brahmin to King Yama. After Yama looked over the brahmin from top to bottom, he directed Yamaduta to release him. Yamaduta told the brahmin that he was a very fortunate man, for his wife had served the traveler at the bright *tritīyā* time during the month of Baisakh. Anybody who serves a guest during that time gains access to the heaven of the god Vishnu (Vaikuntha). When a wife is virtuous, this virtue also spreads to her husband. Then Yamaduta freed him. Whoever performs this brata, whether male or female, goes to heaven after death and remains there.[5]

Hospitality to guests is an important value in Hindu culture: as the proverb goes, "The guest is God." Not only may the guest actually be a god in disguise (there are many ancient stories along this theme) but the guest should be treated as if he or she were divine, as an act of compassion and charity. In this story, the wife follows this value and thus gains virtue and power from her actions.

Women's power traditionally comes from their virtues: earlier bratas made reference to the story of Savitri, whose cleverness saved her husband from death, and here we have Sushila, whose generosity saved her husband from the fires of hell. In Bengali folklore, the wife who is chaste and devoted (called *pativratā* in Sanskrit and *patibratā* in Bengali) has supernatural powers: she can carry water without a vessel and suspend cooking spoons in the air while she attends to other concerns. She has the *śakti,* power, to accomplish things in this and other worlds.

In this brata story, intelligence is not seen as a virtue—the husband possesses it, but he had no corresponding sympathy or compassion. Thus he is condemned, despite his education. Yama is traditionally Lord of the Underworld and also lord of karma. As Yama notes, the husband is freed from the sufferings of hell by his wife's good behavior. He shares in her good karma, even though his own karma is bad. As certain forms of Buddhism follow the notion of transfer of merit, especially by the bodhisattva, so the wife acts as a bodhisattva and transfers her merit to her husband.

Bratas may include a reversal of traditional power relationships: figures who are weak, such as women, become strong and even savioresses. People who make mistakes are not hounded forever by neighbors and by bad karma—they are forgiven, and they learn from their errors of pride and selfishness. Even animals, lowly as they are, hold hidden reservoirs of power.

Some Further Nature Bratas

We have seen bratas that include animals associated with deities, such as Sasthi's cat and Lakshmi's owls. In West Bengal bratas to Manasa the snake goddess have been popular, as have bratas to Subhachani the Duck Mother (also called Subhachani Durga). Both of these goddesses have dark sides but they can be compassionate if they are worshiped and propitiated.

In the case of Subhachani (also called Suvacani, Subachani, and Subhachandi) the Duck Mother, the goddess is symbolized by a human figure with a duck's head, who holds children and nurses them. According to the brata story, a widow and her son lived in the town of Kalinga. They ate one of the king's ducks, which made the king quite angry. However, they prayed to the Duck Mother through the village women and the dead duck was brought back to life. The king was impressed at this and gave his daughter to the widow's son. Everybody involved praised Subhachani, the Duck Mother.[6]

This brata is performed early in the morning, either on a Tuesday or on a Sunday. On the night before, the bratini collects betel nuts, betel leaves, mustard oil, vermilion, and a grinding stone with a sieve. She and any others who wish to participate meet at a crossroad and place the stone and betel nuts and leaves there.

A figure of the goddess is then painted on the stone with a mixture of vermilion and oil. The betel nuts and leaves are offered to potentially threatening spirits known as Thunto Pir and Thinti Pir.[7] A prayer is recited, facing east: "Om! Salutation to Subachani, the honoured of three worlds, the protectress from calamities, who has four faces as red as lotuses, three-eyed, and breasts swollen up with milk, white robed, seated on a swan, possessed of supreme bliss, with Kamandalu in her hand, and with one hand raised in an attitude of compassion and another of chastisement."[8] This is a brata ritual that shows tantric elements (in her multiple faces and abilities invoked in visualization), as well as mainstream Hindu and Muslim influence. Like other aspects of Hinduism, bratas absorb imagery from surrounding traditions.

In other areas, a Subachani ritual is performed for newlyweds. A miniature pond is dug and pairs of ducks and drakes are drawn with rice paste. The tank is filled with milk and married women sprinkle it, after being touched by their feet, onto the heads of the newlyweds to bless them with a child. Here, the life-giving goddess grants pregnancy.

In those parts of West Bengal affected by Assamese religion, there are variations on the brata ritual. Subachani's miniature pond may have water, vermilion, and a few living fish. The duck images are drawn and a variety of other articles are involved: a plantain plant, a clay pitcher with paddy and red cloth, a comb, a mirror, colored thread, vermilion, eggs, pigeons, and a variety of fruits and vegetables. Women listening to the story hold fruit in their hands, and these fruits are later distributed among women whose husbands are alive. Use of animal offerings in bratas is rare, but we see it occasionally. Among tribal communities in Assam, Subachani may be worshiped by the offering of pigeons, ducks, and fowls. According to a text on her worship, the *Subacanī-pūjā-vidhi,* she is the consort of Trilocana, her mount is a cock, and she is fond of blood and raw flesh. In folk songs she is equated with the goddess Kamakhya, and called Kecaikhati (eater of raw flesh); she is also the consort of Shiva as Budha-devata, and in this role she is called Budhi-huvacani.[9] The harmless and benevolent duck-goddess thus shows a different (a more carnivorous) side.

There are also bratas to jackals and vultures. In the month of Ashvin, the brata of Dviti-bahman requires the worship of a female kite and jackal at the river side. The women performing the brata fast all day, then go to the ritual site, which has a bamboo roof hung with garlands, sugar cane, coconut, tulsi plant, and 21 kinds of fruit. The brata story is recited, and the fruit is given to the deity Dviti-bahman, then to the female kite and the female jackal, and then the worshipers.[10] While such creatures are usually understood to be ritually impure and associated with death, in certain bratas they become acceptable, and even sacred.

Sometimes the bratas dedicated to animals are also associated with the Earth goddess. Earth goddesses are important in the agricultural economies of rural West Bengal. P. K. Maity describes the *Saspaṭar brata* observed in honor of the agricultural goddess Bhanjo, in Malda, Birbhum, and Burdwan during the month of Bhadra. In Malda, it involves a mock marriage between the corn seed as bridegroom and the lentil seed as bride, which is enthusiastically celebrated and preceded by a *gāye halud* ceremony in which the bride is annointed with turmeric paste to give her beauty and golden skin. The marriage is accompanied by songs and chants, which continue through the night.[11] This brata ritual involves an imitation marriage for the sake of fertility.

In some areas of Birbhum this brata involves a mock challenge between two neighboring villages. Groups of unmarried girls from both villages collect lumps of earth and stand facing each other, dancing and singing. Eventually one group steps back and the other group takes that group's lumps of earth, returning triumphantly to the village singing victory songs. After that group leaves, the girls from the other village take their lumps of earth and return to their own village. Maity writes that it symbolizes a fight between two rival villages, ending in a victory and a defeat, and that in earlier times men would take part in the mock fight. The collected pieces of earth are taken to a public place for worship, and some village earth is added. A mound of earth resembling the form of a woman is made here. The collected earth is placed on plates with various seeds in a ritual called "the laying of the harvest" (*sasyapata*). The plates are watered until the seeds sprout and grow. The mound of earth is covered by a piece of sari and becomes the goddess Bhanjo. She is offered flowers and the plates of sprouting seed. A priest worships the plants, and in the evening the girls do a circle dance around them, singing folk songs. In the morning, the girls carry the earth figure and the plates with the sprouted plants to the bank of a pond or river, singing songs to Bhanjo. The earth and flowers are consigned to the water, but the plants are carried back to the village, either kept in the thatched roof of the houses or given to the cattle.[12] The earth figure is consigned to the water after the worship, as the goddess has left by then, but the plants are her gift to the town and they remain.

The ritual in Burdwan district to the goddess Bhanjo or Bhajo also involves earth and is performed for a good harvest, but the form made is that of the sky god Indra. Several types of grain are collected by each girl observing the brata, and the majority of them are offered to the goddess Sasthi. The rest are mixed with mustard and earth collected from a rat's hole and kept on a clay plate. The girl waters her seeds until they germinate (and if they germinate rapidly, it is a good omen for the year's crops). An earth mound is made representing the god Indra, and alpana drawings of his thunder are sketched around it. The bratinis place their plates of sprouted plants around the mound, and girls and women between eight and twenty-five years of age do a circle dance around the mound, to songs and music. The next morning the bratinis throw their plates into the river or pond and return home, hoping for a good harvest.[13] The Burdwan style has clearly integrated other deities besides Bhanjo into the ritual: indeed, her role is minor by comparison to the role of the Vedic god Indra. Fertility rituals to the earth goddess often invoke Indra (or Varuna) as god of rain, for rain is vital to the crops. Sometimes he is praised and sometimes he is condemned. Sankar Sen Gupta describes a song the women sing insulting Indra:

> Indra is a god of loose morals, and he was involved in an illicit connection with the wife of his preceptor. It is due to this sin that rains have been stopped. Though he has a thousand eyes, they only see lust, not human suffering. He only pays attention to apsarases, not mankind.[14]

This is a song of accusation: the god had sex with his guru's wife, and he pays attention only to heavenly nymphs. The god has sinned (in a particularly egregious fashion—having sex with the guru's wife is one of the worst possible sins), and he is shirking his obligations to his devotees. It is felt that such insults will disturb Indra, who will then let loose the rains out of embarassment. It shows the folk tendency to insult the gods who are not doing their jobs to get their attention and remind them of their responsibilities.

Another more controversial rain brata involving the Earth goddess used to be performed by the Rajbanshis of Cooch Behar and was known as the Hudma or Huduma brata. In this brata, performed in order to bring rain during a drought, a group of women would go out during a new-moon night. They went out to a field naked and sang songs with sexual content to the god Varuna (Huduma), here invoked as lord of rain. They called upon him to have sex with Prakriti, the earth goddess, and to bring forth children in the form of heavy rains.[15] These songs are still sometimes sung in Bangladesh (once East Bengal), though in recent years they have been changed into love songs. As one song states:

> My loins are stirring, my body is trembling.
> Where should I go to meet my beloved Huduma?
> Now I am unclothed, with my hair hanging loose,
> O Huduma Cloud! Come to satisfy me.
> O Huduma! Come, I am waiting for you.
> My loins are stirring, my body is trembling,
> But my lover is away.
> How can I express my pain?
> Where can I go to be satisfied?[16]

Here the Earth calls to the rain for sexual satisfaction for, without rain, the earth is barren and unsatisfied. The women performing the brata vocalize the Earth's desires, to make sure that Varuna is aware of his neglect. This brata has also been mentioned in several older British accounts of Bengal, and the Victorian writers were clearly scandalized by the sexual implications of the song. However, it was not scandalous for the villages experiencing drought—it was vital to get rain, and this was believed to be one way to do it. As a note, when the women would go out naked at night (as they also did in other rituals for the fertility of the earth, sometimes pulling ploughs beneath the full moon), the men were expected to stay in their homes all night, and not to go out until morning.

This is an older and more primal form of the Earth goddess brata, as opposed to the more modern way it has been handed down for young girls. The modern brata to Prithivi, or the Earth Mother, still focuses on wishes, but here it is said to give a good marriage, and the aspect of desire is not present. According to the *Meyeder Bratakathā*:

THE VOW TO MOTHER EARTH

The Prithivi brata is performed from the last day of the month of Chaitra to the last day of the month of Baisakh and continues for four years. Each day the bratini should draw a picture on the ground. It should be a picture of the earth resting over a lotus leaf. She should gather around it tulsi leaves, white sandalwood, flowers, durba grass, honey, milk, and ghee (clarified butter). She should then chant the following hymn:

> Come, O Earth, and sit over the lotus leaf
> With your conch in your hands.
> I will serve you with cream and milk.
> Let me be the queen of a king.

At the end of four years, the bratini should celebrate by serving brahmins with gold, money, and lotus leaves.[17]

Besides the obvious censoring out of the "stirring loins" for the young women's rituals, we may note brahmanical influence (the bratini must give brahmins gold and money) and a spiritualized earth that rests over a lotus leaf (lotuses grow up through the muck of ponds, and open in light and purity—the earth is thus worshiped as a spiritual entity). We also see the usual desire of the young girl to be a queen.

Another nature brata is to a deity who may be either male or female, Kshetra Thakur (Lord of the Fields) or Kshetra Thakurani (Lady of the Fields). In the version that I have seen, it is dedicated to the Thakurani. This brata is performed in the month of Agrahayana or Baisakh, by a group of women. The deity is worshiped under a tree, with a pitcher holding the branches of three types of trees (arum, jujube, and binca trees) or a green coconut with mango leaves. The story is recited by the oldest woman: a brahmin widow and her child went to her brother, who treated her badly. The widow worked hard in the house, and her son tended his uncle's cattle all day in the fields. Both were allowed very little food, and the child could eat boiled rice and nothing else. As the boy, whose name was Visai, grew up, he ploughed and sowed the land by himself. He became a devotee of Kshetra Thakurani, the Lady of the Fields.

When the widow brought food to her son in the fields, the uncle found out and drove them both out of the house (the uncle had been saving money by not feeding him). They rested under a tree, and the goddess appeared to them in the form of an old woman. She gave the young man magical rice seeds and told him to sell half for food and plant the other half in a nearby empty field. He did so, the next morning there was a full crop of rice. The people who lived in the area were astonished, and told the king what had happened. The king invited Visai and his mother to the palace and offered Visai marriage to his daughter, with a large area of land as dowry. Visai gained wealth and happiness, and rich crops each year, due to the goddess' grace.[18]

Again we have a cruel, greedy brahmin, who casts out his own starving relatives. However, devotion to this local nature goddess (and care for her fields) allowed those in a desperate position to be saved, and rewarded.

Bratas to Gods

There are also bratas to gods, such as Shiva, Krishna, and Surya. Among informants interviewed in West Bengal, the most popular brata to a male god has been the Itu brata, dedicated to Itu, a form of Surya (though some informants had performed this brata, they were uncertain of his identity and guessed that Itu was a form of Shiva or Vishnu).

The story in the Itu brata appears as a sort of Hansel and Gretel story, with the father deserting the two children in the woods. However, rather than a wicked witch they meet a friendly woman in the forest who teaches them the brata, and they are later reconciled with their parents.

As the book states, "This brata is for everybody: young girls, married women, mothers and widows. It gives great happiness. Women should listen with devotion, holding sun-dried rice and grass before a brass pitcher, in the month of Kartik."[19]

The brata should be started on the last day of the month of Kartik (October–November, and continued every Sunday until the last day month of Agrahayan. On that day, Itu should be worshiped after fasting for a day. After the story, everybody is given *sandesh* (tiny cheesecakes) and fruit to eat. The ritual worship should be performed by a brahmin priest.

THE VOW TO THE SUN GOD (ITU BRATA)

There once lived a poor brahmin with his wife and two daughters. One day, he had a great urge to eat pancakes, and with much effort he got the necessary ingredients—rice, oil, coconut, and molasses. He gave these to his wife, and said, "Make me pancakes, but don't give any to anybody else." Then he hid outside the kitchen.

His wife went to the kitchen to make the pancakes, and each one made a sound like "chak-chak-chak." He counted these by tying knots in a rope. When there were no more sounds, he came in and demanded the pancakes. His wife did not know of his trick. She served the pancakes in a stone dish, with a water pot on the side. The brahmin counted the pancakes and found two missing. At first she denied this, then she admitted that the two girls had cried for food, so she gave them each a pancake.

The brahmin became very angry and said, "These girls should live at their aunt's house, they would be better off there."

Early the next morning, he took his daughters toward their aunt's house. But in the dense forest on the way he left his daughters and fled. The girls were lost and began to cry. Then they began to pray.

The next day, as they were looking for a way out of the forest, they saw a house. The woman of the house asked them, "Who are you?" The girls told what had happened to them. The woman saw that they were of brahmin caste, and she invited them into her house. They saw other girls there performing worship before a clay pot and a dish. They asked about this, and the woman said, "They are performing Itu puja, and it requires fasting the day before." The two girls said, "We had nothing to eat yesterday." So the woman taught them to perform the worship.

The sun god saw their devotion and came down to the two girls. He asked what they would like for a boon. The girls folded their hands before him and said, "Our father is poor, give him wealth and sons." The sun god agreed. They continued to pray for their father's happiness.

Meanwhile, the brahmin could see his luck change. His family became rich, and he had many sons. But his wife was not happy—she would think of her daughters day and night, and cry.

After several years the daughters returned, and their parents welcomed them. The household was wealthy, but the girls continued to worship Itu. Seeing them, the brahmin asked, "What god are you worshiping?" The girls told him everything, and the brahmin realized what had happened. From that day on, the brahmin and his wife worshiped Itu. They gave the two daughters to suitable husbands, and the worship of Itu spread through the land.[20]

After looking at this popular brata to a god, one can see why informants emphasized bratas to goddesses. Here we have a greedy, cruel father willing to kill his daughters because they ate a few pancakes, and he is rewarded with wealth and sons rather than punished. When the daughters are given a boon by the god, all they request are benefits for their miserly father. It is thus a curious morality tale, for evil is rewarded, and the girls get very little for their devotion (suitable husbands, eventually). The father never apologizes and gets religion only because wealth comes from it. Itu seems to be primarily concerned with his own worship, and not the welfare of his devotees.

Despite the brahmanical emphasis (brahmin priests are required to perform the worship, the woman in the forest lets the little girls into her house because they are of brahmin caste) this is in many ways an antibrahmanical story. The brahmin father is portrayed as greedy, sneaky, able to get away with attempted murder and still get rewarded in the end. We may also note that, unlike many of the goddess bratas, this is not an original revelation. Itu was already being worshiped by the woman and girls, and the lost girls learned an already-existing set of ritual practices.

There are also bratas dedicated to divine couples, such as the Radha-Krishna brata, which is a more brahmanical brata. Its adventures occur to deities rather than human beings. Here, the god Surya asks Krishna for a daughter who can conquer Krishna—and gets Radha, who later conquers Krishna's heart. It is a far cry from the poor little girls lost in the woods. The Radha-Krishna or Radhastami brata is performed in the month of Bhadra (August–September), and performing it brings blessings from Radha and Krishna. Bratinis should fast for one day and listen to the story.

THE STORY OF RADHA AND KRISHNA

One day, the sage Narada [gossip and troublemaker of the gods] visited the god Krishna. He said, "O Krishna, I have heard that you are going to incarnate in human form. Now tell me about Radha's incarnation."

Krishna said, "All right, sage, you are a great devotee. I'll tell you about it, so please listen. At one time Surya (the sun god) was in deep meditation. The lord of the heavens, Indra, was very surprised at the depth of his meditation. He came to me in fear. I told him not to worry, I would disrupt Surya's meditation [so that Indra did not have to worry about the universe being upset by its power]. Indra felt relieved, and left.

"Then I went to see Surya, who was happy to see me. He said, 'Seeing you has made my meditation a success.'

"I said, 'You are very dedicated, ask me for any boon you wish.'

"He said, 'Lord, I want a daughter, who can overwhelm your own power.' I said, 'So be it,' and gave him the boon.

"Then Surya was born in human form as King Brishabhanu, in the Braj area. He was married to Kirtida, and both were very religious people. In the month of Bhadra, during the full moon part of the month, Radha was born to them (as a daughter). The people of Braj were happy at her birth and threw colored powders to celebrate. They all went to see the baby girl and praised her.

"To celebrate his daughter's birth, Brishabhanu distributed many gifts. After Radha grew up, she worshiped the sun god to have me as her husband. Though we have never been separated for a moment, yet she has suffered for a long time from the illusion of separation."

Narada said, "All right, I have heard of her incarnation. Now tell me how to please her."

Krishna said, "On Radha's birthday, presents should be offered to her and to her relatives. They should be worshiped while fasting, and the next day Vaishnavas should be served. This would please both Radha and myself. Anyone who worships Radha with dedication and who chants my name will be blessed—and also have a good rebirth at Radha's feet. Now I have told you this brata."

Narada practiced this himself, and then (he) spread it to others.[21]

This is a brata story clearly censored for the young girls likely to be reading it. Among Gaudiya or Bengali Vaishnavas, Radha is indeed married—but not to Krishna. Radha and Krishna are unmarried lovers, violating social norms and dharmic expectations. In this version of the story, Radha is a high-caste princess rather than a low-caste milkmaid, and she has one husband and no lovers. This is perhaps a more suitable role model for traditional households than the woman who leaves her husband in bed at night to walk though dark and dangerous forests to the garden where her low-caste cowherd lover waits. This brata also speaks of how welcome the baby girl is to her family—a situation often seen in West Bengal, with its strong tradition of Shaktism or goddess worship, but rare in some other areas of India, especially where dowry is an important part of marriage rituals.[22]

In Bengali Shaktism, the little girl is an embodiment of Shakti, thus welcome in religious households. However, sons bring money into the family at their marriages, as well as wives, so many bratas describe sons as desirable.

Magic and Desire

Some bratas very clearly arise from the folk tradition rather than from brahmanical Hindu tradition—especially those bratas which have chants rather than stories associated with them. These bratas do not involve worship of Hindu deities and focus more on magical imagery. They are usually performed by women. For instance, the Nakhchuter brata (the brata of nail cutting) does not worship a deity but rather creates a woman's image in honey as the ideal woman, empowered by the good fortune of the married woman who is central to the ritual.

The Nakhchuter brata is performed during the Bengali month of Chaitra (March–April), and may be performed for either one year or four years in a row. It is traditionally practiced in West Bengal, in the areas of Navadvipa, Hooghly, and Krishnanagar. The woman who is performing this brata must not cut her nails for a month. On the ritual day (the fourth day of the full moon of Chaitra), she collects a variety of ritual objects and invites a fortunate and respected married woman to participate. A female barber comes to cut the guest's (and later the performer's) nails, rub her feet with a brick (to soften them), and paint the edges of her feet with red *ālta* liquid. The nail parings are saved in a towel. The performer or *bratini* combs the hair of her guest, and puts vermilion on her forehead, and rubs her back until some dirt or dry skin is removed. She shapes this into a tiny doll. The guest puts on a sari with a red border (the typical Bengali sari worn by a married woman) and sits on a wooden stool. The bratini draws the outline of a woman in honey on her guest's back, and touches her with the various ritual objects. She touches her with the local vegetable *parawal* on the area where the honey-woman's eyes would be, and says, "Let my eyes look like the *parawal* cut into halves" (the vegetable is oval shaped and is considered to be an attractive shape for the eyes). The bratini dips the guest's feet into milk and red *ālta* liquid (thus making a pinkish color), and she asks that her skin look like this mixture. The guest holds a small banana, and the bratini asks that her fingers should be as shapely as the banana. Pieces of jute dyed black are placed over the guest's hair, and the bratini wishes that her own hair might look like this.

After this, the objects are placed in a towel, and the guest is fed with certain foods and given gifts (iron and red painted bracelets, vermilion, a mirror, and several other items). The bratini then carries a lit oil lamp on her head to a lake, where she immerses it with the nail parings. This may be performed for four years in a row, and on the fourth year, four married women are invited, have images drawn on their backs with honey, and are given gifts.[23] It may be noted that the requests for light skin and thick hair are not addressed to any god or goddess. Instead, it is the married woman (with her power of auspiciousness) and the image made of honey who hear the prayers. The goal is gaining greater beauty and the love of one's husband, basically through positive thinking and magical ritual. The brata does not involve any stories, fasting, or moral lessons.

Some bratas focus entirely on the desires of the bratini. In the *Daś Putuler Brata* (the brata of the ten dolls), the young woman performing the brata chants the ten wishes, which act as the mantras for the brata. It is traditionally told to girls of five years old, who observe it for four years, from the last day of the month of Chaitra to the last day of Baisakh (roughly, the month of April). Ten figures of dolls are painted onto the courtyard with rice powder and water, and offered flowers, durba grass, and tulsi leaves. The girl or woman then states her desires to these dolls.

In the version of the brata described here, most of the wishes involve imagery from the Ramayana. This implies that the chant may have been imported from outside West Bengal, for the Ramayana is not a major text in this area.[24] Rather than having Sita as an ideal woman or a perfect wife, in West Bengal she is usually understood as an unfortunate woman.

> After I die, I shall be born again in human form.
> I shall be a perfect wife like Sita.
> After I die, I shall be born again in human form.
> I shall get a husband like Rama [who had only one wife].
> After I die, I shall be born again in human form.

I shall get a brother-in-law like Lakshmana.
After I die, I shall be born again in human form.
I shall get a father-in-law like Dasharatha.
After I die, I shall be born again in human form.
I shall get a mother-in-law like Kaushalya.
After I die, I shall be born again in human form.
I shall have sons like Kunti [all of her sons were born alive].
After I die, I shall be born again in human form.
I shall be a cook like Draupadi.
After I die, I shall be born again in human form.
I shall be beloved like Durga.[25]
After I die, I shall be born again in human form.
I shall be as modest as the young green grass.[26]
After I die I shall be born again in human form.
I shall have patience like the Earth.[27]

These ten wishes will be granted if the brata is completed, and an unmarried girl can then expect a happy marriage and a long life, as well as a good rebirth. One associated brata story describes how the daughter of a poor brahmin was able to marry the son of a wealthy landowner due to her performance of this brata. Sometimes these wishes are a separate brata and sometimes they are added to others, such as the Sejuti brata (or *sandhyā-bāti,* a brata to the evening lamp). They may also be added to the *sandhyā-maṇi* brata, when prayers for happiness, peace, and beauty (as well as for 100 burning ovens and a daughter-in-law to preprare the meals) are chanted in the evening, when five stars are seen.[28]

Bratas are performed by women for many reasons. Normally the associated requests are quite positive, but occasionally there are negative bratas, hoping to harm others, which may include destructive versions of the ten wishes.

The older bratas associated with co-wives can be quite negative and serve as a counterweight to the sort of idealization of village religion seen in some writers on folklore. Bratas against co-wives reflect some of the difficulties and stresses inherent in joint families with multiple wives, which used to be seen in West Bengal centuries ago. They are often omitted from the modern brata collections for girls, probably because the dominant marriage forms in modern Hinduism are monogamous, and because they might be seen as bad influences. In the *Meyeder Bratakathā* collection of Bhattacharya and Debi, there are several verses against co-wives. They tend to have repetition and rhyme. For instance, in the following line, the first term is repeated three times, then the fourth rhyming line is chanted.

O stirring spoon (*hātā*), smash my co-wife's head (*māthā*).
O iron bracelet (*beṛī*), make my co-wife a ghost (*cheṛī*);
O wildcat, leave my husband and eat my co-wife.[29]

Other Bratas

There are several which involve birds:

> O bird, bird, bird,
> I am sitting by the river Ganges
> And I see that my co-wife is going to the Ganges [she is dead]

and:

> Mynah, mynah, mynah,
> No co-wife should come here.[30]

and:

> O babui bird, your nest in the palmyra tree is attractive,
> It is also attractive to see my co-wives dying.[31]

In Asutosh Majumdar's version of *Meyeder Bratakathā,* other curses against co-wives are included. This chant is from the *Acinjuti brata,* written in rhymed Bengali verses. It is a magical style of brata, asking household implements, animals, and even the god Shiva to fulfill the bratini's will. While the request to Shiva is fairly benign, the invocations to other beings and objects are more hostile:

> I want to stay under a pipal tree,
> And I want to stab my co-wife
> And put the blood on my feet like *āltā* (red paint).
> And then I want to burn my seven co-wives alive.
> O kitchen knife, come to me, I want to cut up vegetables
> For the funeral (*śrāddha*) rites of my co-wives.
> O broomstick, come to me, and I'll beat my co-wives
> So that they can't live in this country (any more).
> O Shiva, I want a boon that my husband will be a king
> And my co-wife will be my maidservant.
> And let me visit my parents once a year.[32]

In this set of verses, the focus is not on the invocation of deities (though Shiva is mentioned) but rather upon the rhythmic and rhyming expression of desire. Despite its mention of such traditional Hindu concepts as the funeral *śrāddha* rites and the Ganges River, this is a magical style of brata, in structure similar to some spells out of the handbooks on folk tantra (*guṭikā*s). The stresses and difficulties of the polygynous family were well-known in India, especially from previous centuries (today we tend to hear more of the stresses of extended families).

Another chant against co-wives, from the *Bel Pukur* brata, includes the style of the "ten wishes" brata. It could almost be seen as a parody of the Daś Putuler brata, except that the style appears to be quite serious. Again, it is not directed to a deity, though deities are mentioned in passing:

> May I have a husband like Rama,
> May I be chaste like Sita,
> May my husband be happy,
> (And) may my co-wife die.
> May her nose and ears be slit,
> (But) may I get a golden bowl.
> May my husband hate her,
> (But) may I be his best beloved.
> May her path be strewn with thorns,
> (But) may I have a golden son.
> May she be a slave
> While I pass my days in laughter.
> May I be my husband's darling,
> (But) may my co-wife spend her time
> In sweeping the dust-bin . . .
> May three white men take her away
> May she die of consumption.[33]

Again, the style is a rhythmic chant, contrasting the bratini's good fortune with the bad luck of her enemy. These chants are not directed to any deity; they make use of the power (*śakti*) of the bratini herself. It is the bratini's power focused through the chant, which is used as a mantra to bring about the desired state. While most bratas are intended to develop virtues in the young women and inculcate selflessness and generosity, some are intended to respond to the pressures and difficulties of complex families. This particular version is relatively recent, considering the presence of white men.

Some chants involve more positive wishful thinking:

> Now I have jewelry made of paste,
> But I will have jewelry made of gold.[34]

The bratas about co-wives usually involve wishes by women not to have a co-wife in the first place. However, if there is one, the co-wife should be barren, should become a servant, and should die, and the bratini should be able to place her feet in the blood of the co-wife. Clearly, these are not the most brahmanical of bratas (unless one counts the magical rituals of the *Atharva Veda*), and they are understood to be for the good of the bratini and her family rather than for purification or self-sacrifice.

The bratas mentioned thus far are performed by women, primarily by young girls. While in the puranic texts, men performed bratas as well as women, this is not often seen today. Men rarely perform bratas in rural West Bengal, though they do perform other vows known as *mānat*. In this case, a bargain is made with a deity: "If you cure my grandfather of his disease, I will fast for three days." Or, "If you let me graduate even though may grades are failing, I will build you a shrine on my uncle's land." Or, in older times, "If you give me enough money to buy the land I want, I will swing by the hooks for you." Hook-swinging is an ascetic practice that is currently illegal, in which people vow to place hooks in their backs or chests and swing in the air until the hook is ripped out of the flesh. It was primarily performed by men, though sometimes women would take the vows as well. It is still sometimes performed in rural areas, without publicity and with the police elsewhere. Some places are well known for their *manat*s, and have bushes with rocks and bricks hanging by threads, to remind the deity of the agreement. There are temples which have many bushes and trees hung with these reminders, looking somewhat like Christmas trees.

While men rarely perform bratas, I have seen young men creating multi-colored alpana for Durga Puja and other events, especially for welcoming politicians (who are often treated like deities in West Bengal). This is quite nontraditional, both having male artists and using many colors in the rice-paste pictures. It is in a way more brahmanical, though, for in the early Hindu religious texts bratas were intended to be performed by men.

6

Brahmanical Bratas:
The Rituals for Men

The meaning of the term brata (*vrata*) has changed over time. In this chapter, we will examine some of the meanings of the term in Hindu religious literature.

In traditional brahmanical Hindu texts, the Vedas and Upanishads, *dharmaśastras* and *purāṇas*, brata is an important term. In the *Rig Veda,* the term "vrata" was associated with the notion of divine order, and in later Vedic texts, it was used to mean command, religious duty, devotion to a deity, proper behavior, and religious commitment. The term "vrata" appears over two hundred times.[1] It also appears in the later vedic Samhitas, Brahmanas, Upanishads, and Sutras, associated both with cosmic order (*ṛta*) and with a more general concept of order and obligation (*dharma*). The term could refer to jobs, sacrifices, ethical behavior, or taboos.

The Upanishads included ascetic and yogic bratas, which emphasized self-denial. In the law texts, or dharmasastras, bratas focused upon austerities and celibacy. However, by the time of the later texts known as puranas, the term referred to specific rituals, expressing both the devotion and desires of the practitioner.[2]

The practice of bratas in this early Hindu literature is associated with both sacrifice (*yajña*) and austerities (*tāpas*). Sacrifice frequently involved propitiation of a deity in order to secure favor, fame, wealth, strength, protection against enemies, and expiation of sin.[3] The *Rig Veda* includes wishes for long life, children, cattle, and safety from disaster. The term *tāpas* originally meant heat or burning and came later to be understood as penance and devotional fervor, a source of power for accomplishing things in the world. Gods and sages performed great deeds through the use of *tāpas* (for instance, the god Indra conquered heaven by it[4] and the Primal Being practiced *tāpas* before the creation of the world).[5] However, ordinary human beings could also practice austerities and gain deliverance from sins and entrance into heaven. Such austerities as the Krchchacandrayana could make a man invincible, according to the respected commentator Sayana.[6]

In Vedic times, brahmanical bratas were mostly performed by *brahmacārins*, male practitioners otherwise concerned with asceticism and the generation of *tāpas*. Their practices included fasting, isolation, sleeping on the ground or staying awake at night, control of the breath (*prāṇāyāma*), prolonged silence, chastity, and standing for prolonged periods.[7] It was believed the brata was maintained by *tāpas,* as stated in the *Atharva Veda,*[8] and that the bramacarin "should be addicted to *tāpas*" while observing the brata.[9] Such vratas were believed by their practitioners to give magical control over the forces of nature, especially over rain and the fertility of fields.

These bratas were observed for up to a year before new portions of the Vedas were taught to students (some teachings required a full year of bratas and austerities as a prerequisite). These generated the energy or *tāpas* required to understand and be worthy of Vedic knowledge.[10] There were also bratas which preceded the performance of sacrifices. Some of the more ascetic bratas would last for symbolic equivalents of the gestation period (nine months, twelve months, nine days, etc).[11] Such bratas were basically initiatory, performed to prepare the person for ritual brahmanical knowledge (especially to prepare for the initiation ritual or *dīkṣa*). Even until the time of Manu (first to second century B.C.E.), Veda and bratas went together. As the famous Law Book of Manu or Manu Smriti states: "An Aryan must study the whole Veda . . . performing at the same time various kinds of austerities [tāpas] and vows [vratas] prescribed by the rules (of the Veda)."[12] The text also emphasized the use of bratas as penance (*prāyaścitta*) for breaking the rules of proper conduct.

Brahmanical bratas, especially those from Vedic times, involved the generation of *tāpas,* a form of energy. In these bratas, temporary fasting took the place of more extreme measures, such as living in the woods wearing clothing made of bark or leaves, sitting in the midst of five fires (the fifth fire was the hot Indian sun), or living on water and air. Hindu brahmanical bratas were traditionally practiced only by the upper classes, and low-caste practitioners could be punished by death. In the epic text the *Ramayana*, by Valmiki, we see the story of the low-caste (*sūdra*) Sambuka who was killed by Rama because he perfomed *tāpas* hoping to enter heaven with his body. The epic states, "In the three yugas (satya, treta, and dvapara) a *sudra* has no right to perform *tāpas.*"[13] The epics include both abstinence and obligation in relation to bratas, and start to include women as performers of the ritual.

While there are cases of female ascetics (*tāpasīs* or *śramaṇis*) performing austerities in the earlier religious literature, they are rare. Women normally followed the ideal of *pativrata,* in which service to the husband is equivalent to service to a god. Valmiki says that attending to the personal comforts of her husband is the wife's highest religion.[14] Indeed, by this notion a woman could gain entrance into heaven (*svarga*) by serving her husband.

Brahmanical bratas frequently deal with purification and salvation. S. C. Banerjee suggests that Puranic bratas may be classified in two categories, purificatory and devotional. Bratas of purification are performed in order to atone for sins, while devotional bratas are observed by people who seek a definitive object, such as the birth of a son.[15] Vows of purification may also give supernatural abilities: we have such vows as the jatismara brata (silence until the moon rises, which gives the ability to remember past lives), the ardranandakari brata (fasting and worship of Shiva and Parvati, gives afterlife in Indra's heaven), the mandarasasthi brata (worship of the sun with mandara flowers, which gives absolution from all sins), and the rasakalyani brata (bathing a statue of Parvati in ghee gives an afterlife in her heaven).

In the early purana and nibandha texts (500–1000 C.E.), brahmin priests and scholars (*paṇḍits*) become more important, both as ritual specialists and as receivers of gifts. We see the rise of devotion to gods and goddesses and read that women and low-caste people could follow bratas in a limited fashion. Such bratas could give both wealth and long life for this world and liberation in the next world. In the later puranas (1000–1400 C.E.), bratas become very important, and there is elaborate description of their benefits and techniques, as well as who to feed at the end or their performance. The nibandha texts include their structure, involving a statement of intent, bathing, chanting of mantras, sacrifice, worship, *nyāsa* (ritually invoking the presence of gods and goddesses within the performer's body), ritual designs (mandalas, yantras, alpanas), fasting, reading of the brata story, gifts, and concluding rites.

One good way to understand brahmanical bratas is to take a look at a few of them. An important purana in West Bengal is the *Devi Bhagavata Purana,* which is a major text for Bengali Shaktism. It mentions many complicated bratas, clearly intended for brahmin men. One example is the Krichcha-Chandrayana brata, which is described by the god Narayana in this text. He states:

One is to avoid salt, salty or alkaline substances, acid, garlic, turnips, eating in kamsa [metal] vessels, chewing betels, eating twice, putting on impure clothing, intoxicating things and the unsastric nocturnal japam; also one is not to waste one's time over blaming and trying to find fault with the relatives, playing at dice, or talking at random with one's wife. . . . One is to spend one's time in worshiping the Devas, reciting the hymns of praise, and studying the Sastras. One is to sleep on the ground, practice brahmacharyam, and the vow of silence, bathe thrice [per day], not practice anything which befits the Sudras only. One is to worship everyday, make charities duly, and be always happy, recite stotras daily, do occasional Deva worship, have faith in one's Guru and Deva. . . . One is to daily praise the sun, with one's face turned towards Him, do japam before Him; or one is to worship one's own Deity in front of the fire or the image of any god, and do japam simultaneously. The devotee who practices Purascharanam is to bathe, worship, do japam, meditatate, practise Homa, Tarpanam, have no desires and to surrender all fruits to one's own desired Deity, etc. These are necessarily to be observed by him. Therefore while doing Japam [chanting], Homa [sacrificial fire], etc. the devotee's mind is to remain always pleasant and satisfied. One should be ready to practise tapasya [asceticism], to see the Sastras and be merciful to all the beings. . . . First of all shave yourself and have your hair and nails, etc. cut off and bathe and be pure. Then perform the Prajapatya prayaschitta [penance] for one's peace and purification and next do the purascharanam of the Gayatri. Do not speak the whole day and night. Keep your thoughts pure. If words are to be spoken, speak only what you take as true. First recite the Mahavyarhiti [mantra] and then the Savitri mantra with Pranava [Om] prefixed. Then recite the sin-destroying mantra "Apohistha, etc.," and Svastimati Sukta and "Pavamani Sukta." In every action, in its beginning and at its end, one is to understand the necessity of doing the Japam. . . . One is to repeat the Pranava, the three Vyarhitis and Savitri [mantras] one thousand times or one hundred times or ten times. Then offer with water the peace offerings (tarpanam) to the Acharya, Risi, Chhandas, and the Devas. Being engaged in action, do not speak any impure language of the Mlechchhas [foreigners] or talk with any Sudra or any bad person. Do not talk with [one's] wife in the period of menstruation, with one who has fallen, with low-caste persons, with any hater of the Devas and the Brahmanas, Acharyas and Gurus, with those who blame their fathers and mothers; nor show any disrespect to anybody. Thus I have spoken in due order about all the rules of Krichchara vrata.[16]

While ostensibly Narayana described this ritual so that all men could get rid of their sins, it is clear that only a small percentage of Hindus would be capable of performing this brata. The performer needs knowledge of a wide variety of Sanskrit mantras, stanzas, and Vedic chants, as well as the ritual techniques for Homa fires and offerings to the ancestors. He would also need knowledge of Sanskrit for studying various traditional sacred texts. The performer of this brata is told to be respectful toward everybody—however, he should not speak with any low-caste person or even with his wife if she is menstruating. Caste hierarchy is simply accepted without question here, as is brahmanical knowledge gained by initiation. Because of the focus on Sanskrit knowledge, it is clear that this brata is intended for men rather than women (who were not generally taught Sanskrit). However, we may note that later puranas included simplified bratas for women, as religious rituals that can be performed as a part of family life.

In general, puranic bratas focused less on stories and morality tales and placed more emphasis on mantra and ritual detail. Puranic texts were widely accepted and assumed to have an authoritative origin; thus there was less need for stories to justify the brata rituals.

On the general topic of bratas, the god Brahma states to the sage Vyasa in the *Garuda Purana:*

O Vyasa, hear me discourse on the mode of performing a variety of Vratas, which can win the good graces of the god Hari, who blesses the performer with all his cherished boons in return. A Vratam signifies an act of living in conformity with the rules of conduct and self-control, as laid down in the Sastras. The Vratam is but another name for penance (Tapasya). A Vrati (performer of a Vratam) is under the obligation of observing specific rules

of conduct and self-control. He should bathe thrice every day during the en-
tire term of the Vratam, and sleep on the bare ground, contented and controlled in his mind and senses, and renouncing all talk with women, Sudras,
and degraded persons. . . . He should not take any thing out of a bowl of Indian bellmetal, nor consume any potherbs, nor take honey grain, and Ko-
radushaka, nor chew any betel leaf on the day of breaking his fast, nor take
his meals in another's house on the occasion. A fast is vitiated by using flowers, perfumes, unguents, collyrium, a toothbrush, a new cloth, or an article
of ornament. A Vrati should wash his mouth with the Pancha-gavyam in
the morning before breaking his fast. The merit of a fast is destroyed by
gambling, by indulging in day-sleep or in sexual intercourse, and by con-
stantly drinking water on the day of its breaking. . . . The Vratas may be
practised though a proxy, but penances must be personally performed. A
vow broken through anger, greed, or incontinence should be atoned for by
a three-day fast and a clean shave of the head. The performance of a Vratam
may be delegated to one's son in case of one's ill health. A Brahmana, swoon-
ing away in the course of a Vratam, should be enlivened with milk and cold
applications.[17]

Some brahmanical bratas include their own advertising, as in this description of Ekadashi brata (here, the Ekadasi Vratam, a fast for a day during the wax-
ing moon, which is intended to destroy sin or bad karma):

This Ekadasi Vratam destroys all sins as surely as a bad son brings ruin on
his family, a false wife brings death and disgrace to her husband, a false min-
ister brings confusion to his king, and a pious act dispels the gloom of iniq-
uity. As knowledge dispels nescience, as purity removes the impurity of the
heart; as truth conquers untruth, and reverence, irreverence; so this Vratam
annihilates all kinds of sin. As surely as cold removes heat, as profligacy destroys a stored-up treasure, as bragging of it destroys the merit of a gift, as
worldliness destroys penance, the Ekadasi Vratam destroys all sin. As surely
as a son is ruined without good education, cattle are destroyed by straying
far from the folds, as a peaceful temperament is ruffled by anger, and as ex-
penditures without income destroy one's wealth, so the Ekadasi Vratam destroys all kinds of sin. As surely as a motive destroys the merit of an act, as
knowledge destroys nescience, this Vratam destroys all kinds of sin. The
sins that are attached to acts of Brahmana slaughter, wine-drinking, gold-
stealing and defiling the bed of a preceptor, when simultaneously done, are
absolved by performing the Ekadasi Vratam in its true spirit. . . . Neither
the holy shrines of Kurukshetra, Prabhasa and Naimisha, nor the sacred
rivers, the Ganges, the Yamuna, the Kalindi and the Sarasvati, can rank
equal in merit with the Ekadasi Vratam. Neither the practice of charity and
philanthropy, nor meditation and burnt offerings can vie with the Vramam

under discussion, in respect of merit and sanctity. The merit of an Ekadasi Vratam weighed in balance with that of making a gift of the whole world immensely outweighs the latter.[18]

However, most brahmanical vratas limit their own advertising and are simply rules, and if they are properly followed, great things can result. For instance, in the *Garuda Purana,* Brahma states:

> One should perform a Vratam on the day of the eighth phase of the moon and break his fast on the night of the vow. He who continuously practices the Vratam for a year and closes it by making the gift of a cow to a Brahmana, is elevated to the status of an Indra after death. This Vratam is called Sadgati Vrata. The same Vratam practised on the day of the eighth phase of the moon's increase in the month of Paush is called the Maha Rudra Vratam.[19]

Some puranic vratas are intended for nobles and kings and require a fair investment of money and time. They often seem more like typical ritual worship (*pūjā*) than austerities. The *Garuda Purana* describes the Ajachita Vrata to Durga, to be performed on Mahanavami day, as revealed by Brahma:

> A king wishing victory over his royal adversaries should practise an Ajachita Vratam from the previous sixth day of the moon's increase, and close it on the abovesaid day [the ninth day of the moon's increase] with rites of Japa and Homa, and by feasting the unmarried virgins. The worship should be conducted by reciting the "Durga, Durga Rakshini Svaha" (Oh, Durga, Durga, obeisance to Durga, the protectress) Mantra. . . . A new wooden temple should be constructed, and a golden or silver image of the Goddess Durga should be worshiped therein, on the eighth day of the moon's increase. As an alternative, the Goddess should be invoked and worshiped at the head of a spear, or at a swordblade, or in a book, picture, or a mystic diagram. The Goddess should be contemplated as respectively holding a human skull, a dagger, a bell, a mirror, a Tarjani, a bow, a banner, a small drum, and a noose in her left hands, and a spear, a club, a trident, a thunderbolt, a sword, a mace, an arrow, a discus and a rod in her right. . . . The votary should observe a fast on the eighth day of the moon's increase after having worshiped the Goddess in an image, or in a divine sandal, or in water. A bull buffalo, five years old, should be sacrificed at the close of the night, and the blood of the offering should be offered by duly reciting the "Kali, Kali" Mantra.[20]

Brahma also notes that the Digdashami Vrata to Durga on the tenth phase of the moon's increase, concluded by making to brahmins a gift of ten cows as well as golden images of the presiding deities of the quarters of heaven, gives the practitioner rulership of the universe.[21] Such gifts are important in the brahmanical style of bratas, as S. C. Banerjee states:

> Gifts to Brahmanas on the day of Vrata occupy a very prominent position and an extensive space in the the Puranic literature. No Vrata can be regarded as complete without such gifts. . . . among the things to be given away to Brahmanas gold ranks highest. Besides golden images of certain deities in particular Vratas one has to offer gifts of flowers, chariots, fish, horse, lion and trees, etc., made of gold. Next to gold is the cow. In most of the Vratas the gift of cows or of bulls forms an essential part of the ceremony. Metals such as silver, copper, etc., may also be given in certain cases, especially when the donor is rather poor. Besides these specific gifts, all the articles of worship in a Vrata are to be made over to Brahmanas. It is noteworthy that in addition to the above things, daily necessaries like salt, paddy, sugar, cloths, blankets, beds, fan, umbrella, footwear, etc., are also to be given to them. That the Brahmanas made the Vratas an instrument for earning their livelihood seems evident from such injunctions as make the comparatively rich people give away land or sometimes even a whole village to Brahmanas in order to ensure the full benefit of Vrata. . . . In making gifts one is strongly and repeatedly warned against what is very frequently called Vitta-Sathya. The term may be translated as deceitful economy; that is to say, spending less money than what is allowed by one's income. One resorting to Vitta-sathya with regard to gifts is doomed to hell.[22]

In this type of brata, not only are expensive gifts demanded for brahmins, but performers of bratas are threatened with hell if their gifts are not expensive enough to satisfy the brahmins. Banerjee also suggests that the bratas acted as a "bulwark for the Brahmanas" against such rival faiths as Buddhism and Jainism (by giving them money and social status), and that the fasting and continence were ways to protect the Hindu society from Tantric influence.[23]

The puranas (or "ancient stories") include ritual, philosophy, myth, and genealogies of kings and deities, among other topics. Puranic bratas require correct timing, a clear statement of intent (reason for the brata, and the goal), ritual bathing, mantras, homa fire sacrifice, worship with mandala or yantra, fasting, charity (generally to brahmins), and concluding rites.

While some scholars understand the brahmanical bratas and the folk bratas to be opposed, there is some overlap between them. Puranas are enormous collections of information, and sometimes a folk brata can slip in. The *Bhagavata Purana* is a major brahmanical text for the Bengali or Gaudiya Vaishnavas. It talks about the life and adventures of the god Vishnu/ Krishna. However, we may note that in Book Ten of this text, the gopis perform a brata to the goddess Katyayani, hoping to gain a good husband (the best possible one being Krishna, of course, as this is a Vaishnava text). The gopis bathed, ate pure food, made an image of the goddess out of sand, and worshiped it with incense and gifts. Calling her by the titles Ruler of the Universe, Yogini, and Bhadrakali, they ritually worshiped the goddess. They then went swimming in the Yamuna River, leaving their clothes on the river bank. At this point, Krishna and his friends come and steal their clothes.[24] This event is quite famous, though both the performance of the brata and the presence of Krishna's friends tend to be left out in the popular versions of the story.

Both forms of bratas are intended to lead to happiness, in this world or the next.

7

Conclusion

In recent years, much writing on India has focused on colonialism and its legacy. There is concern with the deleterious effects of British imperialism in the economic and political spheres and on the psychological and social outlook of the "subaltern" or Indian native.

Such debates are important in urban areas and among high-caste, educated Indians. But when we observe the rural areas, we see that the majority of people are more concerned about other issues. For them, the legacy of British oppression is much less important than the legacy of caste oppression. Problems for villagers who are not high caste come from landowners following the old Muslim Zamindari system (where villagers must work another's land and never to own it), and from some caste Hindu developers who take over tribal and village land using false claims and deception. There have also been largely low-caste and tribal villages where the brahmins in charge outlaw local religious rituals in the name of "proper" Hindu religious practice, and this has caused great resentment.[1]

Some of the most important tensions in rural West Bengal are between castes (which still exist, though prejudice based on them has been banned in the Indian constitution) over proper marriage and over land ownership and inheritance. While ideally there is arranged marriage, there is often marital separation, divorce, and remarriage in villages (which would be quite scandalous for the higher castes and urban elites). Women also share more labor and have more independence than in urban areas. Sexuality is more free, as there is less concern in low-caste village and tribal women with Hindu ritual purity and impurity rules than we see in high-caste urban women.[2]

Some of the underlying tensions between high-caste brahmanical Hinduism and low-caste folk Hinduism are reflected in the brata stories. These two types of Hinduism are not mutually exclusive—brahmin priests can be found chanting Sanskrit in villages, and women from villages who marry into more urban settings often take local rituals along with them. There is also a rising middle class, though the majority of India is low-caste and rural. Still, these types of Hinduism contain different notions of authority structure and often different deities and styles of worship. Much research has been done on the relationship of the "great tradition" and "little tradition" and the process of "Sanskritization," and the ways that these styles interact and blend. To unite them can be a challenge, and the bratas are one way that this has been done. These stories both link and contrast various aspects of these types of Hinduism.

While the brahmanical bratas of the puranas and dharmasastras generally describe preexisting rituals, most folk bratas give new revelations, describing the salvific action of a deity in a historical situation. While brahmanical bratas emphasize the high gods of Hinduism, of Kailash or Goloka or Indra's heaven, the folk bratas emphasize more regional deities and have a greater focus on goddesses. While brahmanical bratras emphasize knowledge of Sanskrit language and literature, folk bratas are performed in the vernacular and may be understood by children. While brahmanical bratas tend to be practiced by individuals, and limited by caste and initiation, folk bratas tend to be communal, shared with a group of people of varying ages and experiences. While brahmanical bratas enforce the rules of traditional Hindu dharma, folk bratas ignore such details, having deities who overlook violations of religious rules (such as eating beef) and protect the violators. One brata even portrays traditional dharmic rules as conflicting with the god Dharma himself.

While the focus of the older brahmanical bratas is obedience to gods and to tradition, folk bratas have other emphases: community, self-expression, respect for the natural world. Folk bratas have traditionally served a number of functions in West Bengal:

1. Bratas encourage community and shared activity between women at different stages of life. There are bratas that include the ritual worship of young girls (*kumārī pūjā*) as incarnations of Durga or Lakshmi, and bratas which involve the ritual worship of young married and older women, appreciating their luck in living happily and having a healthy family. The life stages of youth, motherhood, and old age are shown respect through ritual worship and offerings (usually of food, red *sindūr* powder, and saris). The different stages of life are shown to be valuable to the community, and group and individual friendships are supported. Such support is important, for much work in rural India is shared.

2. Bratas encourage artistic creativity in the designing and painting of *ālpanā* pictures. These designs are unique to each artist, and young girls can get a reputation in the villages for the beauty, complexity, and originality of their alpana pictures. Artists can be appreciated without the necessity of expensive supplies and gallery shows, and modern events can be incorporated into the pictures (today, some pictures include trains, airplanes, and political events). The pictures can show the creation of religious worlds in physical form, as well as comment on the social world around the artists. Some more modern alpanas show social and political satire in their illustrations and allow women a political say in regions where this is difficult for them.

3. Bratas encourage closeness to nature, as may be seen in stories of people who are rewarded for taking good care of plants and animals. Some bratas involve the creation of and caring for miniature forests, groves, and lakes. Those who respect nature, watering tulsi plants and feeding hungry baby birds, get their dreams fulfilled. As in many European folk-tales, the compassionate hero or heroine who has pity on suffering plants and animals is rewarded.

4. Bratas encourage showing concern for and caring for others, especially family members. Fasting and prayers are often performed for the sake of others, so that the husband and children may be healthy, or that they will have luck in the future, or gain wealth if they are poor. While some bratas are for the happiness of the woman performing them, most focus on the happiness of those around her. It emphasizes happiness found in the social world, rather than in a supernatural or heavenly world.

5. Bratas encourage concentration in girls who are often unschooled, and give positive expectations and optimism for the future. The various bratas of the ten wishes emphasize the future identity and situation of the bratini, she will be strong as Durga and patient as the earth. They may also bring encouragement, for the heroines and goddesses suffer as human beings do, having to work at menial jobs and to be despised and misunderstood, yet they are able to overcome their difficulties. Both deities and heroines within the bratas can act as role models for the bratinis.

6. Bratas articulate underlying power struggles between husbands and wives, between co-wives, and between relatives of the extended family. Women can see that they are not alone, that their problems are shared by others, and these problems can be portrayed in the context of the bratas. Bratas can "change one's luck," and also change the understanding of problems. For instance, several bratas reveal the hidden virtues of wives and daughters to the men in the family who might otherwise not notice them.

The influence of bratas on luck is important, because in traditonal Bengali Hindu life the woman is the luck of the house. When a new bride comes into her husband's joint family household, if everybody is healthy and there is extra food and money, the bride is said to be like Lakshmi and to bring good fortune with her. This makes her a valued member of the household. However, if she enters the house and soon the family members get sick, or the husband loses his job, then she is said to bring bad luck to the house and to be like Alakshmi, the goddess of poverty and misery. Her status in the household will then be low, for she will be blamed for the family's misfortunes.

It is difficult to guarantee luck, but bratas are believed to help in this area. By pleasing a deity, the woman may be blessed and thus more likely to bring good fortune with her through life. Even if the bratas do not work, at least she can be seen as making an effort to bring good luck. If good fortune does occur, then the bratas (and the bratini) can claim credit for it.

Bratas are also a form of religious play—some informants said that they saw the performance of bratas as a game when they were young and only realized their significance when they were older. It is religious action that can be either serious or enjoyable, and those bratas with images can be interpreted by young girls as playing with dolls, pretending to have a family, or worshiping kind deities. The practices can involve play, or love, or faith, or worship, or even anger, depending on the individuals and the context.

The understandings of bratas for women has changed because the role of women has changed over the history of Hindu religion. During the Vedic period, women had access to religious education, participated in sacrificial ritual and feeding the ancestors, and some wore a sacred thread and were scholars and philosophers (*paṇḍitā*s). Many women had high religious status in the community. However, the rise of ascetic religion caused women to be seen as temptations and as sinful, especially by men trying to be celibate. Women came to be compared to low-caste people, associated with impurity, lack of intelligence, and lustfulness.

Because women were considered so inherently sinful, they therefore were given less free access to religious rituals and their benefits; the famous writer Manu stated that no woman could perform a sacrifice, brata, or fast without her husband's permission.[3] Manu felt that no woman should ever be independent from male control.

However, we also have the dichotomy between "good woman" and "bad woman." The "good woman" is the wife and mother, who brings luck to the house and is to be respected by her husband and children. She is the *pativratā*, who serves her husband as if he were a god and performs all household work perfectly and without stress or complaint. The virtuous woman is perfectly adapted to following her proper obligations (*dharma*).

The "bad woman" is the woman who does not accept the marriage arranged for her by her parents or who is unfaithful to her husband, perhaps with a series of lovers. Dharma texts call such women weak, promiscuous, and untruthful. Because their emotions and desires are uncontrolled, they would not have the necessary discipline for ascetic ritual, and the ritual instruction would be wasted on them.

The mild forms of asceticism (such as the *nirjala brata* of fasting without food or water for a day, or not eating hot food or taking a bath for a day) associated with some bratas can also be understood as a game rather than as a sacrifice. One female head of an ashram told of how she learned to enjoy such ascetic practices in her youth and to see them as a game, because they showed that she could be strong, and they were done in a community of people that she loved.[4] It trained her for the sacrifices needed later on in life and taught her not to be selfish.

However, while in the Hindu yogic tradition asceticism with its extremes of renunciation should ideally separate the practitioner from worldly involvement, the asceticism in bratas is intended to influence the world, leading to such worldly goals as wealth, fertility, a good husband, and health of the family. They bring the girl or woman closer to the family and the world, not further away. Some folk bratas seem to depend on the yogic ascetic notions of *tāpas* and folk understandings of female power or *śakti,* while others depend on devotion to deities and receiving the deity's grace.

In the idea of *tāpas,* the meditations and sacrifices performed give power to the performer through the energy that is suppressed and controlled rather than expressed (for perception and interaction with objects of desire means the loss of energy, and the yogi must draw his or her energy inward, as a tortoise draws in his legs). In the idea of *śakti,* the young girl or woman naturally possesses some of the essence or power of Sakti as the universal goddess of creation and destruction, and her virtue, concentration, and selflessness (especially as shown in the performance of bratas) increase that power.

In later devotional bratas when women became devotees, a deity is invoked—a god or goddess—and the story becomes a sort of a moral tale of how a good person would act toward that deity. If a person acts in a positive way, he or she gains blessings from the deity. In other bratas, no deity is involved. The performer simply has intense wishes, often combined with imagery (pictures, statues, natural objects). The underlying dynamic appears to depend on the bratini's *śakti* or personal power, as well as a personal relationship to a deity.

Śakti may be personal or impersonal. As personal power, *śakti* may be increased by meditation and ascetic practice. Such *śakti* is the basis of the power of female ascetics, the *yoginī*s, *sannyāsinī*s, and *sādhikā*s of West Bengal. However, among female householders, it may be increased by following dharmic rules, or moral rules, such as eating only pure foods, showing reverence and respect toward husband and family, and keeping a clean and orderly household. A housewife's power, or *śakti,* is gained by her devotion to husband and family.

Śakti is also an impersonal power, the force of nature or the underlying power of the universe. Both meditation and perfect adherence to dharma may bring the person to a greater realization of that impersonal aspect as well. According to one informant, a Bengali housewife living in Calcutta, *śakti* is the universal force of movement. As she stated:

> When I meditate, I think about the power within me, how it moves my hand, my body. I ask what this power is, how does it come to be within me? I do not read and write, that is not my way. Life is so short, it just wastes time. The root of this power is *śakti,* without it nothing moves. The energy which moves the stars, the energy in my body, on this I do meditation (*dhyāna*).[5]

While some bratas are consciously performed in order to gain *śakti,* more often there are more mundane goals. Sometimes bratas are performed to teach girls lessons. As Shudha Mazumdar states in her memoirs of her life in West Bengal:

There was another *brata* that Mother made me undertake. When roused, I was the unfortunate possessor of a fiery temper and stinging tongue, which in Mother's opinion was most unbecoming in a maiden and would mean endless sorrow for me at my future father-in-law's house. At the same time, I was always blurting out things that were better left unsaid. When reprimanded, I justified myself with, "But, it is true, Mother, so why should I not say it?" According to her, there was a proper time and place for truths, but I could never gain her perspective. After losing an argument, my elder sister once retreated with the comment that my tongue was not to be wondered at since I was born under the sign of Cancer, and she warned Mother of the dire consequences in store for me if nothing were done about it.

So, Mother at last decided upon the *Madhu-Sankranti* brata. For two successive years on the last day of each month, I had to give a small new bell-metal bowl of *madhu* [honey] and a silver coin to a holy man, and then take the "dust of his feet" in salutation. It was hoped that by his blessings I would gain a honeyed tongue.[6]

From a feminist perspective, the brata tradition is both good and bad for women. It is good because it encourages female community and mutual respect for women of all ages and stations in life. By worshiping both young girls and old women, bratas demonstrate that both of these often-ignored groups have value and should be appreciated. Because the brata tradition is a form of folk religion, it ignores the traditional caste hierarchy of male brahmin priests in favor of informal, often low-caste priestesses, auspicious married women, who become the teachers and ritual specialists of the tradition. It is primarily the women who carry down the stories and teach the practices and not the men. It is also primarily women who learn and perform them.

However, there are aspects of the bratas which would be negative from a feminist viewpoint. While some bratas tell women to disagree with their bad husbands and act independently, most stories reinforce traditional values, in which women are submissive, self-sacrificing, and obedient. Such values allow women to accept social situations in which they are often understood as second-class citizens, having less food and medical care than males, and fewer choices in life. Many young women in rural West Bengal grew up eating less food than their brothers, or eating their leftovers, and they greatly resented this lack of respect.

We may also note that the "Sanskritization" or professionalization of the bratas has worked against the older women who used to teach and practice them, for they are no longer considered expert enough to lead them in the urban areas. Instead, we have male brahmin priests who tell these stories. As Rowlands notes, in these "brata analogues" (imitations of folk bratas by brahmins, who change them around and place themselves in a position of importance), the older women are no longer honored, and only the priests are honored.[7]

There has been some debate among scholars whether women perform bratas for the sake of others, while men perform them for themselves (especially for their own salvation), or whether women perform bratas for their own welfare. This issue seems to depend on the type of brata performed. In those bratas that emphasize love as a value, they are performed to bless the family, or those suffering, or to help a young women get a good husband or a married woman get children. (Is getting a husband or child good for herself, or for someone else?) Even wishing for the welfare of others in the family may be called selfish, as it makes one's life easier. It depends on one's understanding of altruism. It does seem clearer that those bratas performed in order to influence afterlife are focused on the individual.

In those brahmanical bratas requiring Sanskrit training and initiation, there is less emphasis on compassion—the brata is a purification rite to prepare the man for mantras and classical knowledge. His goal is enlightened detachment, *mokṣa,* not selfless love or *prema.*

Sometimes we have mixtures, where worldly fortune is gained through ascetic practice (*tāpas*). In Sanskritic-style bratas, it is generally a male god who knows the tradition, which can work oddly sometimes. For instance, in the Haritalaka brata, we have Parvati asking her husband Shiva to tell her what rituals she has performed in order to gain him as a husband. One would think that she would know, since she performed them. However, in this case, Shiva tells her what she already did, and thus becomes the source of this ritual knowledge.[8]

While the cultural stereotypes have women seeking love and men seeking knowledge, and these are certainly present, they are not always accurate images. There are exceptions. I have encountered female *sādhikā*s who had brahmanical training and knew Sanskrit mantras and who sought *mokṣa.* I have also met male Bengali Vaishnavas who sought perfect love of Krishna as a religious goal and dedicated their time to serving others and developing devotion in themselves.

While Manu, the famous medieval writer of law codes, felt that no women should perform a brata independently of her husband, I have met women who chose their religious rituals on their own and did not ask their husbands for permission. Instead, they simply announced their intentions. There are also unmarried women of all ages who perform bratas to attain their chosen goals.

I have heard many religious reasons for the performance of bratas by women: to gain the blessings of gods and goddesses, to keep the husband and family safe, to attain peace and security. However, one informant, who told me of the bratas she performed during her childhood, described a pragmatic rather than an altruistic reason for performing the rituals. Ironically, fasting allowed the girls to eat a good meal afterwards:

> My grandmother used to do bratas, and I did them too, especially to Mangala—chandi, Shiva's wife. I was really young then. I fasted all morning, and at 1:00 P.M. an elderly lady would read the story of the brata. We would

listen, standing with flowers in our hands. Nearby would be a pitcher (*ghaṭ*) with five or seven mango leaves, and on it would be a green coconut daubed with vermilion. We would listen to the stories of the bratas and the *Chandi mangala,* and when they were over we would have a feast. We would eat plenty of food, cooked and uncooked, vegetarian and without salt. There were lots of sweets. I think the reason why women liked bratas so much was that traditionally, the men got all the best food, and the women only got the leftovers. But on brata days, the women got the best food. It was allowed because it was for the benefit of the family. This is one reason that women always did bratas—the men had to give them good food at the end.[9]

We see in the practice of bratas a mingling of rituals. The brahmanical bratas are highly ritualized, beginning with a statement of intent and involving mantras, purifications, prayers, and gifts of gold or valuables to brahmins. The folk bratas are more informal, taught to young girls by older women, and often revealed by local goddesses who seek worship. They may have stories, or rituals, or both. When the types are mixed, we see the worship of local goddesses mixed with ethical stories following Hindu dharmic ideas, meant to instill moral behavior in the listeners. As in the case of many religions, the folk rituals become justified by the ethical teachings.

Folk bratas are not organized by institution or sacred place, they tend to be more oriented toward home and family. While they often emphasize the submissive role of women, there are many stories that emphasize the strong and independent aspects of women, especially in those bratas in which wives save their husbands from hell or other dangers due to their innate virtue or having gained power or a boon from some deity. They work in contradictory ways, acting both to socialize the young woman into mainstream Hindu society and to subtly point out its limitations and problems. They show the difficulties of life, in magical and fairytale form, and emphasize the importance of religious faith.

Bratas are an important means of establishing relationships between humans and gods or nature, as well as repairing a relationship gone bad. They are a method of bringing harmony to the universe, and overcoming alienation of humans from divine and natural forces.

Bratas have acted to maintain an authoritative role for women within the religious tradition of Hindu worship, in a situation where most priests were male. Today, the practice of bratas is declining, at least partly due to the influences of science and Westernization. West Bengal is a Communist state and a great threat is Communist materialism, which understands religious belief to be both superstitious and a threat to the state. Now businesses from the West, television, and computers are filtering in, even to the rural areas. It will be interesting to see if the brata tradition can survive the modernization of India.

Notes

Chapter 1. Folk Hinduism in West Bengal

1. W. L. Smith, *The One-Eyed Goddess: A Study of the Manasa Mangal* (Stockholm: Almqvist and Wiksell, 1980), p. 74.

2. *Adhyatma Ramayana,* trans. Swami Tapasyananda (Mylapore: Sri Ramakrishna Math, 1985), V.27–32, pp. 26–27.

3. Interviews, villagers in Birbhum, 1994.

4. We see this is the story of Tarakhya Devi, in Aśok Mitra, *Pascimbangera Puja Parban O Melā* (Delhi: Controller of Publications, 1992), vol. 4, p. 49.

5. As in the story of the goddess Adya Shakti and the saint Annada Thakur, a popular Bengali saint story.

6. Bholanath Bhattacharya, "The Spring Time Fair of Makar Chandi of Makardah," *Modern Review,* Calcutta, Sept. 1971, p. 174.

7. R. M. Sarkar, *Regional Cults and Rural Traditions: An Interacting Pattern of Divinity and Humanity in Rural Bengal* (New Delhi: Inter-India Publications, 1993), p. 134.

8. Interview, Elementary school teacher, Bolpur, 1994.

9. Sarkar, *Regional Cults,* p. 134.

10. Sarkar, ibid., p. 139.

11. Nanimadhab Chaudhuri, "Cult of the Old Lady," in *Journal of the Royal Asiatic Society of Bengal,* Letters, vol. 5, 1939, pp. 417–18.

12. Chaudhuri, ibid., p. 419.

13. Chaudhuri, ibid.

14. Mitra, *Pascimbangera Pūjā Pārban O Melā,* vol. 4, pp. 271–72.

15. Sibandu Manna, *Mother Goddess Candi: Its Socio-Ritual Impact on the Folk-life* (Calcutta: Punthi Pustak, 1993), p. 199.

16. The anthropologist describing this ritual does not discuss its meaning, but one might speculate that thread linking people with a sacred tree could be appropriate for weavers.

17. Manna, ibid., pp. 157–60.

18. Manna, ibid., p. 108.

19. Himangsu Mohan Ray, *Savara, the Snake Charmer* (Calcutta: ISRAA, 1986), p. 135. Chandi is here called the Hadi's daughter, or the daughter of a low-caste person. It is sometimes said that Chandi once took on human form as a member of the Hadi caste, thus blessing all members of that caste. This chant is re-

translated, in order to get the original rhythm and imagery (the book translated it into a prose paragraph).

20. Ray, ibid., p. 138.

21. "Three women beaten for 'witchcraft'" written by an unidentified staff correspondent, *Amrita Bazar Patrika,* dated March 7, 1994.

Chapter 2. The Folk Goddess Tushu, Her Festival, Songs, and Brata

1. This was stated by Surajit Sinha, ex-head of the Eastern Division of the Anthropological Survey of India, and supported by Ranjit Bhattacharya, current head of that division of the Anthropological Survey. Interview, Calcutta, 1994.

2. This was discussed by Satyakam Sengupta, an anthropologist and folklorist who did research in over 400 villages in West Bengal. Interview, Calcutta, 1994.

3. Kiśalaya Ṭhākur, "Uṭsaber Lokāyata Anginaya," *Deś,* September 1987, p. 80.

4. P. K. Bhowmick, *Socio-Cultural Profile of Frontier Bengal* (Calcutta: Punthi Pustak, 1975), p. 269.

5. Suhrid Bhowmik, *Tushu Songs,* translated with James D. Robinson (Mecheda: Marang Buru Press, 1990), p. 1. This is the only book in English that I have located about Tushu songs. Additionally, the folklorist Asutosh Bhattacharyya states in his *Folklore of Bengal:* "There is a folk ritual in the district of Purulia and its neighbourhood observed by the womenfolk during the Bengali month of Paus after harvesting is over. It is known as the worship of Tusu, an unorthodox harvest goddess. Songs of the different realistic aspects of domestic life rather than on the divinity of Tusu are sung on this occasion. This is the most important regional festival of the area and the songs sung on this occasion are some of the finest specimens of Bengali folk-songs" (Asutosh Bhattacharyya, *Folklore of Bengal,* New Delhi: National Book Trust, 1983).

6. Surajit Sinha, Biman Kumar Dasgupta, and Hemendra Nath Banerjee, "Rituals in Agriculture," chapter 5, in *Bulletin of the Anthropological Survey of India,* vol. 10, no. 1, Jan. 1961, p. 32.

7. Salil Mitra, *Tuṣura gān* (Palasi/Hooghly: Bhaktirani Mitra, 1376 BS/1969), p. 12.

8. According to the dowry system, which is still prevalent in India, the bride's family must give money and gifts to the groom's family, with whom the daughter will be living. The dowry system has been a great cause of problems in India, and many families have gone into debt trying to get husbands for their daughters. It is a major reason for daughters being devalued among mainstream Hindu families. In the bride-price system, on the other hand, daughters represent wealth coming into the family, and are accordingly highly valued.

9. We see the mood of blame in many Shakta poets. One famous example is Ramprasad Sen, who wrote of how the Mother forced him to starve, to suffer, and to be devoted to her without worldly reward. Usually songs that include the bhava of blaming and condemnation of the goddess end with a reconciliation, and the poet stating his willingness to accept whatever the goddess chooses for him.

10. Sung by Pashupati Mahato, December, 1993. He is the leader of the Jharkhand singing group "Suvarnarekha," and has sung many of these songs for Tushu festivals.

11. Sung by Pashupati Mahato, December, 1993.

12. Rādhāgovinda Māhāto, *Jhārkhander Loka-Samskṛti* (Calcutta: Bhairav Pustakalaya, 1379 BS/1972), p. 218.

13. Āśutosā Bhattācārya, *Bāṅglār Loka-Sāhitya,* (Calcutta: Calcutta Book House, 1985), p. 94.

14. Sung by Basanti Mahato, Calcutta, 1994.

15. Ṭhākur, "Uṭsaber Lokāyata Anginaya," p. 80.

16. Bhaṭṭācārya, *Bāṅglār Loka-Sāhitya,* p. 94.

17. Sung by Purnima Sinha, Calcutta, 1994.

18. Mitra, *Tuṣura gān,* p. 12.

19. Yajñiśvara Chaudhuri, *Bardhamān: Itihās o Samskṛti* (Calcutta: Ānandamayī Chaudhuri, 1991), vol. 2, p. 339. This song is clearly not mainstream Hindu, for a married woman would find it extremely difficult to leave one marriage for another.

20. The term used in the song is *puin śak,* a leafy vegetable that grows in Bengal. The seeds are also eaten.

21. Rabindranāth Sāmanta, *Tuṣu brata o gīti samīkṣa* (Calcutta: Pustak Bipani, 1385/1978), p. 117, song no. 68. There is a long history in Bengal, and in India generally, of stress between new daughters-in-law and the mothers-in-law with whom they go to live at the time of marriage. As a Bengali proverb states:

> My mother-in-law died in the morning.
> If after taking my lunch, I get time,
> I shall cry for her in the afternoon.

22. Sāmanta, ibid., p. 108.

23. Retranslated from the Bengali, in K. C. Shasmal, *The Bauris of West Bengal: A Socio-Economic Study* (Calcutta: Indian Publications, 1972), p. 201. Tushu songs are sung widely, both inside of Purulia and outside.

24. Māhāto, *Jhārkhander Loka Samskṛti,* p. 221.

25. Mitra, *Tuṣura gān,* p. 9.

26. Sudhīr Kāran, *Sīmānta Bāṅglār Lokjān* (Calcutta: E. Mukherji, 1965), p. 345, no. 28.

27. Ṭhākurdas Sahat, ed., *Janapriya Ṭusu Sangīt* (Purulia: Rajak Press, n.d.), p. 8.

28. Sahat, ibid., p. 8. Note: I have reversed the order of the last two stanzas.

29. Sung by Basanti Mahato, Calcutta, 1994.

30. Sung by Pashupati Mahato, remembering encounters in his youth. Interview, Purulia, 1994.

31. Bhowmick, *Tushu Songs,* p. 60.

32. Ṭhākur, "Uṭsaber Lokāyata Anginaya," p. 80.

33. Binaya Māhāto, *Lokāyata Jhārkhand* (Calcutta: Navapatra Prakāśan, 1984), p. 249.

34. Mitra, *Tuṣura gān,* p. 3.

35. Note: the English word is used in the song, adopted from the foreign landlords.

36. Māhāto, *Jhārkhander Loka Saṃskṛti,* p. 223. Note: In the temple of Rankini Devi in Mahula village, the statue of the goddess stands on the prone body of Shiva and is offered puja on Tuesdays and Saturdays. The statue is believed to be currently alive and was installed by a tantrika named Rama Brahmachari in the midst of a dense forest for worship. A town has grown up around it. The temple has a history of human sacrifice, and a case of such offerings was reported in the newspapers in 1837, where the temple priest went to the temple in the morning and found pools of blood all around, as well as large offerings, ornaments worth thousands of rupees, and 1,000 red jaba (hibiscus) flowers. A headless corpse was found shortly thereafter in the river, and the village elders felt that some raja must have performed the sacrifice to help his spiritual practice (sādhanā), for the offering showed great wealth. The police said that it looked like another case of human sacrifice (there were several previous cases in the temple), but were unable to find who had done it. For details, see Aśok Mitra's *Pascimbangera Pūjā Pārvana O Mela,* Bardhamān District, p. 101.

37. Amal Kumar Das and Manis Kumar Raha, *The Oraons of Sunderban* (Calcutta: Bulletin of the Cultural Research Institute, Tribal Welfare Dept., Government of West Bengal, Special Series no. 3, 1963), p. 323. Retranslated.

38. Das and Raha, p. 321. This poem is retranslated from the Bengali, to improve the grammar and expression.

39. Das and Raha, ibid., p. 323. Retranslated.

40. Das and Raha, ibid., p. 324. Retranslated.

41. Das and Raha, ibid., p. 325. Retranslated.

42. Das and Raha, ibid., p. 326. Retranslated.

43. Interview, Calcutta, 1994.

44. A particular area of concern was a marriage tradition used by the Mahato people and not accepted by the Indian government. In this tradition, girls were married to trees before they were married to human husbands. In this way, they would never become widows and would always be close to nature. However, this was frequently dismissed as superstition by brahmanical Hindu officials, which the rural people took as a religious insult. Interview, Pashupati Mahato, Calcutta, 1994.

45. Pallab Sengupta, *Pūjā Pārban Utsakathā* (Calcutta: Anup Kumār Mahīnda, 1990), p. 168.

46 Bhowmick, *Tushu Songs,* p. 5.

47. Chaudhuri, *Bardhamān,* p. 338

48. Chaudhuri, ibid., p. 338.

49. P. K. Maity, *Folk Rituals of Eastern India* (New Delhi: Abhinav Publishing, 1988), pp. 20–21.

50. This devotional brata involves a set of vows and requests, a sort of exchange between goddess and devotee. The worshipper asks for boons and promises in return to serve the god or goddess in certain ways.

51. Rādhikā, or Rādhā, is the beloved of the Hindu god Krishna. In this case, the tribal goddess is being associated with the Hindu tradition.

52. *Sindūr* or vermilion is a red powder, worn on a woman's part to represent luck and fertility and to signify that her husband is alive. No widow may wear *sindūr.* Both the iron bracelet (a sort of "lightning rod" that keeps bad luck away from one's husband and family) and the *sindūr* powder are symbols of a happy marriage.

53. Chaudhuri, *Bardhamān,* p. 339.

Chapter 3. What Is a Brata?

1. Sankar Sen Gupta, *Folklore of Bengal—A Projected Study* (Calcutta: Indian Publications, 1976), Appendix, Table 4.3.

2. Sanskritists have variously derived the term "vrata" from the roots "to choose," "to protect," and "to proceed." Emotions ran strong, and there was a public debate over the term that took place in a variety of Indological journals. For further details, see Mary McGee, *Feasting and Fasting: The Vrata Tradition and Its Significance for Hindu Women* (ThD thesis, Harvard University, 1987), p. 16.

3. Pandurang Vaman Kane, *History of Dharmaśastra: Ancient and Medieval Religious and Civil Law* (Poona: Bhandarkar Oriental Research Institute, 1958/1930), vol. 5, part 1, p. 8.

4. Kane, ibid., p. 11.

5. Kane, ibid., p. 27.

6. Anne Pearson, *Because It Gives Me Peace of Mind: Ritual Fasts in the Religious Lives of Hindu Women* (Albany: State University of New York Press, 1996).

7. See Susan Wadley, "Hindu Women's Family and Household Rites in a North Indian Village," in Nancy Falk and Rita Gross, *Unspoken Worlds: Women's Religious Lives in Non-Western Cultures* (San Francisco: Harper and Row, 1980), p. 109.

8. See Raheja, Gloria, and Ann Gold, *Listen to the Heron's Words: Reimagining Gender and Kinship in North India* (Berkeley: University of California Press, 1994), p. xxxiv.

9. See Laxmi G. Tewari, *A Splendor of Worship: Women's Fasts, Rituals, Stories and Art* (New Delhi: Manohar, 1991).

10. These include Dakshinaranjan Mitra-Majumdar's *Bāṅglār Bratakathā,* Abanindranath Tagore's *Bāṅglār Brata,* Asutosh Kaviratna's *Meyeder Bratakathā,* and books of the same title by Āśuṭosa Majumdār and Bibhūtibhūṣhaṇ Bhaṭṭācārya.

11. A Shakta priest at a Kali temple in Bolpur sometimes instructed girls in performing bratas. He said that he made extra money on the side from teaching bratas to girls—it was a sort of secondary job for him. Interview, 1994.

12. This derivation is from Tapon Mohan Chatterji, *Alpona: Ritual Decoration in Bengal* (Calcutta: Orient Longmans, 1965/1948), p. 31.

13. Chatterji, ibid., note, p. 30.

14. Chatterji, ibid., p. 33.

15. Shib Chunder Bose, *Hindoos As They Are* (Calcutta: S. Newman and Company, 1881), p. 35.

16. Joguth Chunder Gangooly, *Life and Religion of the Hindoos, with a Sketch of My Life and Experience* (London: Edward T. Whitfield, 1860), p. 95.

17. Mary McGee, *Feasting and Fasting: The Vrata Tradition and Its Significance for Hindu Women* (ThD thesis, Harvard University, 1987), p. 226.

18. Pupul Jayakar, *The Earth Mother: Legends, Ritual Arts, and Goddesses of India* (San Francisco: Harper and Row, 1990), pp. 15–16.

19. Jayakar, ibid., p. 26.

20. Jayakar, ibid., p. 128.

21. In her research on Banaras, Pearson notes the importance of brahmin pandits for more complex *pūjā* rituals in bratas involving *upācāras,* homa fires (in which ghee is offered into the fire, accompanied by Vedic mantras), havans (in which herbs are poured into the fire, also accompanied by Vedic mantras). They also are well fed and receive money and other offerings. See Pearson, p. 290. She also notes the frequent presence of pandits telling the brata stories, and writes that almost all women that she interviewed in Banaras regularly called on a priest to be present at some bratas. See Pearson, p. 294. This would be quite unusual for West Bengal, especially rural Bengal, where the local women are the authorities.

22. J. Helen Rowlands, *La Femme Bengalie Dans la Litterature du Moyen-Age* (Paris: Adrian Mainonneuve, 1930), pp. 50–51.

23. Eva Maria Gupta, *Brata und Alpana in Bengalen* (Wiesbaden: Steiner, 1983), p. 4.

24. Pearson, ibid., p. 129.

25. P. K. Maity, *Folk Rituals of Eastern India* (New Delhi: Abhinav Publications, 1988), p. 3.

26. S. R. Das, *Folk Religion of Bengal: A Study of the Vrata Rites* (Caluctta: S. C. Kar. 1953), p. 12.

27. Das, ibid., p. 45.

28. Cited in Maity, ibid., p. 6.

29. Sankar Sen Gupta, *A Study of the Women of Bengal* (Calcutta: Indian Publications, 1970), p. 100.

30. Sen Gupta, ibid., p. 100.

31. Sudhansu Kumar Ray, *The Ritual Art of the Bratas of Bengal* (Calcutta: Firma KLM, 1961), p. 12.

32. Ray, ibid., p. 10.

33. Ray, ibid., p. 14.

34. Ray, ibid., pp. 33–36.

35. Ray, ibid., p. 49.

36. Chatterji, ibid., p. 4.

37. Shudha Mazumdar, *Memoirs of an Indian Woman,* ed. Geraldine Forbes (London, Me. E. Sharpe, 1989), p. 17.

38. Mazumdar, ibid.

Chapter 4. Some Bengali Bratas to Goddesses

1. Paṇḍitprabar Gopālcandra Bhaṭṭācārya and Ramā Debī, eds., *Meyeder Bratakathā: Baromaser* (Bibidh Purānokta O Prachalit Nanabidh Brater Niyam, Brataphal, Bratakathā Prabhṛti Ekathe), Calcutta: Nirmal Book Agency, n.d. I translated most of these stories in West Bengal with the help of a research assistant, Soumen Dutta. This source will be abbreviated from now on as MB.

2. P. K. Maity, *Folk Rituals of Eastern India,* p. 31.

3. She thus identifies with the major character in the story, Kalavati, who is a perfect daughter and wife.

4. It is considered an ideal death for a wife to die before her husband (thus showing that she does not have bad karma that harms or kills her husband), and to leave a son, which shows her fertility and blessings from the gods.

5. MB, pp. 6–8.

6. Das suggests that the frog offering as the ending of the brata is a plea for rain and cites various examples of frog worship. He notes that, in Assam, a mock marriage is celebrated between two frogs, moving the female frog seven times around the male, followed by the women participants singing and dancing. This frog marriage is performed to bring rain. See S. R. Das, "A Note on Rain-Making Rites," p. 142.

7. MB, pp. 9–11. Here Durga reveals the brata. Durga in folk religion is often worshiped as a vegetation goddess, especially near or within trees, as Bana Durga or Durga of the Forest.

8. MB, pp. 57–61.

9. Sudhir Ranjan Das, *Folk Religion of Bengal (A Study of the Vrata-Rites).* Calcutta: S. C. Kar, 1953. Part 1, no. 1, p. 23.

10. Das, ibid., pp. 24–25.

11. It is often striking in these brata stories to see the one-dimensional nature of the characters. Here a family member has died and there is no response of grief—the family simply says that she got what she deserved for not worshiping Lakshmi. The focus is on moral lessons rather than character development, as we often see in folktales.

12. MB, pp. 186–90.

13. MB, pp. 96–101.

14. A common theme in European folklore is the boy (often a youngest son) who is good-hearted but unfortunate. He goes out into the world to seek his fortune, and he is kind to animals along the way. They later help him when he is in danger and bring him good fortune, often in the form of wealth and/or marriage with a princess.

15. MB, pp. 78–80.

16. MB, pp. 133–36.

17. MB, pp. 102–104.

18. MB, pp. 165–68.

19. It may be a mark of the imaginative nature of this story that a brahman who got his son married in hopes of a dowry would give up the chance to ask for wealth from the king.

20. MB, pp. 122–27.

21. MB, pp. 105–109.

22. In the village setting where arranged marriages predominate, the young bride must live in the joint household of her husband's family and must often act as a servant to her mother-in-law. It is said that the new wife often has a difficult time adapting to the ways of her new husband's family, and according to a Bengali proverb, it is "as difficult as cooking iron beans."

23. MB, pp. 52–57.

24. MB, pp. 68–69.

25. Maity, *Folk Rituals of Eastern India,* pp. 95–96.

Chapter 5. Other Bratas: Women, Nature, Gods, and Magic

1. MB, p. 25.

2. MB, p. 27.

3. *Kumārī pūjā* is the traditional worship of a young virgin girl, with offerings of food, incense, and saris. It is most widely practiced by members of the Shakta tradition in Bengal, often during the festival of Durga Puja.

4. MB, p. 33.

5. MB, pp. 38–39.

6. Ray, *Ritual Art of the Bratas of Bengal,* p. 15.

7. While pirs are wise and saintly figures in Islamic Sufism, they are not always seen as positive among Hindu groups.

8. Maity, *Folk Rituals in Eastern India,* pp. 70–71.

9. Hemanta Kumar Sarma, *Socio-Religious Life of the Assamese Hindus: A Study of the Fasts and Feasts of Kamrup District* (Delhi: Daya Publishing, 1992), pp. 119–20.

10. A. N. Moberly, "Miniature Tank Worship in Bengal," in *Journal of the Asiatic Society of Bengal,* vol. 2, 1906, p. 495.

11. Maity, *Folk Rituals,* p. 17.

12. Maity, ibid., pp. 17–18.

13. Maity, ibid., p. 19.

14. Sankar Sen Gupta, ed., *Rain in Indian Life and Lore* (Calcutta: Indian Publishing, 1963), p. 65.

15. Sibendu Manna, *Mother Goddess Candi,* p. 40. This same ritual was described by several members of the East India Company; also described in *North Indian Notes and Queries.* As in the case of human sacrifice, there are writers today who claim that such rituals never occurred, and were only figments of the imagination of British observers.

16. Slightly rephrased, from Mustafa Zaman Abbasi, ed., *Folkloric Bangladesh* (Dacca: Bangladesh Folklore Parishad, 1979), p. 41.

17. MB, p. 15.

18. This story comes originally from Sen Gupta's *Rain in Indian Life and Lore,* and was cited in Maity, ibid., pp. 13–14.

19. MB, p. 127.

20. MB, pp. 127–29.

21. MB, pp. 89–91.

22. Two important rituals associated with marriage are dowry and bride price. In the dowry tradition, money is paid by the bride 's family for the largest wedding gift, the money with which the newlyweds will start out their marriage (even if they do go to live with the husband's family in an arranged marriage, as often happened). In the tradition of brideprice, the groom's family pays the money for the wedding gift. In regions where the bride's family loses money on the marriage of the girl, girls are frequently devalued and parents often hope for male children. However, in regions where bride price is prominent and the groom's family loses money on the wedding, parents often look forward to having female children.

23. Charulal Mukherjee, "Bratas in Bengal: A Cult of Beauty," *Man in India,* vol. 30, April/September 1950, pp. 67–69, for a detailed description of this brata.

24. There are some Bengali versions of the *Ramayana,* whose plots differ from those of northwestern India. For instance, according to the *Krittivasa Ramayana,* Sita turns into Kali and she kills the thousand-headed Ravana (called Mahiravana).

25. As a note, in the versions of this brata that come from northwestern India, Durga is "courageous" rather than "beloved."

26. Or according to some versions, as cool as the Ganga.

27. MB, pp. 17.

28. J. Helen Rowlands, *La Femme Bengalie dans la Litterature du Moyen-Age* (Paris: Librairie d'Amerique et d'Orient, 1930), p. 133.

29. MB, p. 147–48.

30. MB, p. 147.

31. Āśutoṣ Majumdār, *Meyeder Bratakathā* (Calcutta: Deb Sahitya Kutir, 1991), p. 112–15.

32. Majumdār, ibid., p. 115.

33. Moberly, "Miniature Tank Worship," p. 502. The article included both the original Bengali and a translation; I added the parentheses, as the translator included a few terms that were not in the original chant.

34. MB, p. 148.

Chapter 6. Brahmanical Bratas: The Rituals for Men

1. P. V. Kane, *History of Dharmasastra,* V, 1:4.

2. Mary McGee, *Feasting and Fasting,* p. 1. This dissertation is a very good source for information on classical bratas.

3. Mansukh G. Bhagat, *Ancient Indian Asceticism* (New Delhi: Munshiram Manoharlal, 1976), p. 101.

4. *Rig Veda,* X.167.1, cited in Bhagat, ibid., p. 105.

5. *Rig Veda* X.129.3, cited in Bhagat, ibid., p. 105.

6. Bhagat, ibid., p. 105.

7. Walter O. Kaelber, *Tapta Marga: Asceticism and Initiation in Vedic India* (Delhi: Sri Satguru Publications, 1989), p. 18.

8. *Atharva Veda* 10, 7, 1, cited in Kaelber, ibid., p. 18.

9. Quote from the *Gobhila Gṛhya Sutra,* 3, 2, 17, cited in Kaelber, ibid., p. 18.

10. Kaelber, ibid., p. 68.

11. Kaelber, ibid., p. 69.

12. Manu 2.164–65. Cited in Kaelber, ibid., p. 68.

13. *Ramayana* VII,75.25, cited in Bhagat, Ibid. We may note that Kali Yuga is not mentioned here, so there may be more ascetic rights for sudras in the modern world. However, in India the affirmative action for low-caste and outcaste people emphasizes jobs and civil rights more than ascetic rights.

14. *Ramayana* II.24.28, cited in Bhagat, ibid., p. 265.

15. S. C. Banerjee, "Puranic Basis of the Vratas Mentioned in Bengal Smṛti," *Indian Culture: Journal of the Indian Research Institute,* vol. 8, no. 1, 1946, p. 35.

Notes

16. *The Srimad Devi Bhagawatam,* trans. Swami Vijnanananda (New Delhi, Oriental Books Reprint Corporation/ Munshiram Manoharlal, 1977), chapter 23, book 11, 21–42, pp. 1128–29.

17. *Garuda Puranam,* trans. Manmatha Nath Dutt Shastri (Varanasi: Chowkhamba Sanskrit Series Office, 1968), pp. 372–74. Chowkhamba Sanskrit Studies, vol. 67.

18. *Garuda Puranam,* ibid., pp. 370–71.

19. *Garuda Puranam,* ibid., p. 303.

20. *Garuda Puranam,* ibid., pp. 386–87.

21. *Garuda Puranam,* ibid., pp. 388–89.

22. S. C. Banerjee, "Puranic Basis of the Vratas Mentioned in Bengal Smrti," Ibid, pp. 36–37.

23. Banerjee, ibid., pp. 38–39.

24. *The Bhagavata Purana,* trans. Ganesh Vasudeo Tagare (Delhi: Motilal Banarsidass, 1978), Ancient Indian Tradition and Mythology Series, vol. 10, part 4, pp. 1395–96.

Chapter 7. Conclusion

1. For instance, according to informants in the Purulia area of West Bengal, the Kurmi/Mahato people had a tradition of having the bride marry a tree before marrying the groom (thus, she would never be a widow for as long as the tree stood). This was made illegal, and they have been protesting that decision as an infringement of their religious rights.

2. In such areas, not only is there little tension with the West and its historical interactions with India (about which many villagers know little), in many villages there is also harmony between Hindu tradition and Islam. This is noteworthy because much modern literature emphasizes their struggles. I have interviewed Hindus who told me that Islam was not another religion (*dharma*), but rather another lineage (*sampradāya*), and thus quite compatible with Hinduism. They have Muslim friends and participate in each other's rituals.

3. Manu, Manusmṛti, V. 155. See the *Laws of Manu,* trans. Georg Buhler, in The Sacred Books of the East Series.

4. Interview, Archanapuri Ma, Jadavpur, 1994.

5. Interview, Mrs. A. K. Sinha, Calcutta, 1994.

6. Mazumdar, *Memoirs of an Indian Woman,* p. 24.

7. Rowlands, *La Femme Bengalie,* p. 133.

8. For a full translation of this brata, see Pearson, *Because It Gives Me Peace of Mind,* pp. 239–42.

9. Interview, Professor, Viśvabharati University, Shantiniketan, 1994. The issue of food and women is complex in India, for women traditionally have control of the food and determine its distribution. It is unusual for a male to spy on

123

the kitchen, keeping track of the food (as did the evil father in the Itu brata story). I have had adult female informants speak of their hunger as children in rural villages and how both father and mother preferred to feed sons. However, I have also had adult male informants speak of how women use cooking as a weapon and how their wives starved them into submission. Because there are no stores for packaged food or restaurants in villages, men must eat with their families (or at least people in the same caste group). It is shameful for men to admit that their wives refuse to cook for them, and they often do not wish to go to the houses of others and admit the situation to outsiders. Food can become an issue of threat and negotiation, and several of the brata stories show conflicts associated with food.

Bibliography

Abbasi, Musfafa Zaman, ed. *Folkloric Bangladesh* Dacca: Bangladesh Folklore Parishad, 1979.

Adhyatma Ramayana, trans. Swami Tapasyananda. Mylapore: Sri Ramakrishna Math, 1985.

Banerjee, S. C. "Puranic Basis of the Vratas Mentioned in Bengal Smrti." *Indian Culture: Journal of the Indian Research Institute.* Vol. 8, no. 1, 1946, pp. 35–44.

Basu, Sajal. *Jharkhand Movement: Ethnicity and Culture of Silence.* Shimla: Indian Institute of Advanced Study, 1994.

Bhagat, Mansukh. *Ancient Indian Asceticism.* New Delhi: Munshiram Manoharlal, 1976.

Bhagavata Purana, trans. Ganesh Vasudeo Tagare. Delhi: Motilal Banarsidass, 1978. Ancient Indian Tradition and Mythology Series.

Bhaṭṭācārya, Āśutoṣa. *Bānglār Loka-Sāhitya.* Calcutta: Calcutta Book House, 1985.

Bhattacharyya, Asutosh. *Folklore of Bengal.* New Delhi: National Book Trust, 1983.

Bhattacharya, Bholanath. "The Spring Time Fair of Makar Chandi of Makardah," *Modern Review,* Calcutta, September 1971.

Bhaṭṭācārya, Paṇḍitprabar Gopālcandra, and Ramā Debī, eds. *Meyeder Bratakathā: Baromaser (Bibidha Purāṇokta O Prachalit Nānābidha Brater Niyama, Brataphala, Bratakatha Prabhṛti).* Calcutta: Nirmal Book Agents, n.d.

Bhowmick, P. K. *Socio-Cultural Profile of Frontier Bengal.* Calcutta: Punthi Pustak, 1975.

Bhowmick, Suhrid, and James Robinson, trans. *Tushu Songs.* Mecheda: Marang Buru Press, 1990.

Bose, Shib Chunder. *Hindoos As They Are.* Calcutta: S. Newman, 1881.

Chatterji, Tapan Mohan. *Alpona: Ritual Decoration in Bengal.* Calcutta: Orient Longmans, 1965 (1948).

Chaudhuri, Nanimadhab. "Cult of the Old Lady," in *Journal of the Royal Asiatic Society of Bengal,* Letters, vol. 5, 1939.

Chaudhuri, Yajñiśvara. *Bardhamān: Itihāsa O Samskṛti,* vol. 2. Calcutta: Ānandamayī Chaudhuri, 1991.

Das, Amal Kumar, and Manis Kumar Raha. *The Oraons of Sunderban.* Calcutta:

Bulletin of the Cultural Research Institute, Tribal Welfare Department, Government of West Bengal, Special Series no. 3, 1963.

Das, Sudhir Ranjan. *Folk Religion of Bengal: A Study of the Vrata Rites.* Part 1, no. One. Calcutta: S. C. Kar, 1953.

Gangooly, Joguth Chunder. *Life and Religion of the Hindoos, with a Sketch of My Life and Experience.* London, Edward T. Whitfield, 1860.

Garuda Puranam, trans. Manmatha Nath Dutt Shastri. Varanasi: Chowkhamba Sanskrit Series Office, 1968. Chowkhamba Sanskrit Studies, vol. 67.

Gupta, Eva Maria. *Brata und Alpana in Bengalen.* Wiesbaden: Steiner, 1983.

Jayakar, Pupul. *The Earth Mother: Legends, Ritual Arts and Goddesses of India.* San Francisco: Harper and Row, 1990.

Kaelber, Walter O. *Tapta Marga: Asceticism and Initiation in Vedic India.* Delhi: Sri Satguru Publications, 1989. Sri Garib Dass Oriental Series no. 106.

Kane, Pandurang Vaman. *History of Dharmaśastra: Ancient and Medieval Religious and Civil Law.* Poona: Bhandarkar Oriental Research Institute, 1958 (1930), vol. 5.

Kāraṇ, Sudhīr. *Sīmānta Bāṅglār Lokjān.* Calcutta: E. Mukherji, 1965.

Karlekar, Malavika. *Voices from Within: Early Personal Narratives of Bengali Women.* Delhi: Oxford University Press, 1991.

The Laws of Manu, with Extracts from Seven Commentaries, trans. Georg Buhler. The Sacred Books of the East Series. New Delhi: Asian Educational Services, 1977 (1886).

Mahapatra, Sitakant. *Unending Rhythms: Oral Poetry of the Indian Tribes.* New Delhi: Inter-India Publications, 1992.

Māhāto, Binaya. *Lokāyata Jhārkhand.* Calcutta: Navapatra Prakāśan, 1984.

Māhāto, Rādhāgovinda. *Jhārkhander Loka-Samskṛti.* Calcutta: Bhairava Pustakalaya, 1972.

Maity, Pradyot Kumar. *Folk Rituals of Eastern India.* New Delhi: Abhinav Publications, 1988.

Majumdār, Āśutoṣa. *Meyeder Bratakathā.* Calcutta: Deb Sahitya Kutir, 1991.

Manna, Sibendu. *Mother Goddess Candi: Its Socio-Ritual Impact on the Folk-life.* Calcutta: Punthi Pustak, 1993.

Mazumdar, Shudha. *Memories of an Indian Woman,* ed. Geraldine Forbes. London: M. E. Sharpe, 1989.

McGee, Mary. *Feasting and Fasting: The Vrata Tradition and Its Significance for Hindu Women.* Harvard ThD, 1987.

Mitra, Aśok, ed. *Pascimbangera Pūjā Pārban O Melā.* Vol. 4. Delhi: Controller of Publications, 1992.

Mitra, Salil. *Tuṣura gān.* Palāsī/Hooghly: Bhaktirani Mitra, 1969.

Moberly, A. N. "Miniature Tank Worship in Bengal," in *Journal of the Asiatic Society of Bengal,* vol. 2, 1906.

Mukherjee, Charulal. "Bratas in Bengal: A Cult of Beauty," in *Man in India,* vol. 30, April/September 1950.

Pearson, Anne Mackenzie. *Because It Gives Me Peace of Mind: Ritual Fasts in the Religious Lives of Hindu Women*. Albany: State University of New York Press, 1996.

Raheja, Gloria Goodwin, and Ann Grodzins Gold. *Listen to the Heron's Words: Reimagining Gender and Kinship in North India*. Berkeley: University of California Press, 1994.

Ray, Himangsu Mohan. *Savara, the Snake Charmer*. Calcutta: ISRAA, 1986.

Ray, Sudhansu Kumar. *The Ritual Art of the Bratas of Bengal*. Calcutta: Firma KLM, 1961.

Ray, Sukumar. *Folk Music of Eastern India (with special reference to Bengal)*. Calcutta: Naya Prokash, 1988.

Rowlands, J. Helen. *La Femme Bengalie dans la Litterature du Moyen-Age*. Paris: Librairie d'Amerique et d'Orient, 1930.

Sahat, Ṭhākurdas, ed. *Janapriya Ṭusu Sangīt*. Purulia: Rajak Press, n.d.

Sāmanta, Rabindranāth. *Tuṣu Brata O Gīti Samīkṣa*. Calcutta: Pustak Bipani, 1978.

Sarma, Hemanta Kumar. *Socio-Religious Life of the Assamese Hindus: A Study of the Fasts and Feasts of Kamrup District*. Delhi: Daya Publishing, 1992.

Sarkar, R. M. *Regional Cults and Rural Tradition: An Interacting Pattern of Divinity and Humanity in Rural Bengal*. New Delhi: Inter-India Publications, 1993.

Sengupta, Pallab. *Pūjā Pārban Utsakathā*. Calcutta: Anup Kumar Mahinda, 1990.

Sen Gupta, Sankar. *A Study of the Women of Bengal*. Calcutta: Indian Publications, 1970.

Sen Gupta, Sankar. *Folklore of Bengal—A Projected Study*. Calcutta: Indian Publications, 1976.

Shasmal, K. C. *The Bauris of West Bengal: A Socio-Economic Study*. Calcutta: Indian Publications, 1972.

Sinha, Surajit, Biman Kumar Dasgupta, and Hemendra Nath Banerjee. "Rituals in Agricultre," in *Bulletin of the Anthropological Survey of India,* vol. 10, no. 1, January 1961.

Smith, W. L. *The One-Eyed Goddess: A Study of the Manasa Mangal*. Stockholm: Almqvist and Wiksell, 1980.

Srimad Devi Bhagavatam, trans. Swami Vijnanananda. New Delhi: Oriental Books Reprint Corporation/ Munshiram Manoharlal, 1977.

Tewari, Laxmi. G. *A Splendor of Worship: Women's Fasts, Rituals, Stories and Art*. New Delhi: Manohar, 1991.

Ṭhākur, Kiśalaya. "Uṭsaber Lokāyata Anginaya," *Deś,* September 1987.

Wadley, Susan. "Hindu Women's Family and Household Rites in a North Indian Village," in Nancy Falk and Rita Gross, *Unspoken Worlds: Women's Religious Lives in Non-Western Cultures*. San Francisco: Harper and Row, 1980.

Index

(Note: Important terms and deities have diacritical marks included here)

/